TEACH ME TO PLAY
a first bridge book

by
JUDE GOODWIN
DON ELLISON

Published by
PANDO PUBLICATIONS
Roswell, Georgia

TEACH ME TO PLAY

a first bridge book

Pando Publications
540 Longleaf Drive
Roswell, Georgia 30075

ISBN 0-944705-01-4

Oh! you know
I just want to see —
you laughing.
DUNCAN BRAY

This book
is lovingly dedicated
to
Sky and Jewel

The authors would like to give a special
thank you to Don Richards
for his help and advice.

TABLE OF CONTENTS

welcome to the World of BRIDGE

This world is an exciting place
with many different and friendly people.
No matter where you go in the world of Bridge,
if you play bridge, there are no strangers.

AND...

People play Bridge everywhere.
They play it in China, in Africa, in Australia, in England.
They play it in kitchens, in basements, in churches,
in hotels, in campers, in castles.

ALSO...

Rich people play Bridge. So do poor people, little people,
famous people. Kings, generals, movie stars, athletes.
People in your neighborhood play Bridge, drink tea, and eat
goodies served on china plates. People play Bridge on
huge cruise ships slicing through oceans, all heading for
exotic islands. People rent large rooms and have clubs
where they play bridge day and evening. Thousands
will meet to play at tournaments, filling convention centers,
arenas, and ballrooms with color and laughter.

At the Bridge table, wherever you go, however you look,
whatever you do,
you are all the same, HUMAN BEINGS
PLAYING BRIDGE...

all you need

TO PLAY BRIDGE:

★ A Deck of Playing Cards

★ 4 People

★ This Book

You can play Bridge on a table, on the floor, on a bed, in a car, on a train, on a jet, at a picnic, on a stage, in a dugout, in a treehouse, under a blanket, on a raff, under a sundeck.

THIS IS YOUR BOOK.

With this book, (and maybe some help from a special friend, who already plays Bridge!), you can learn enough about the game to sit down and start to play.
And you'll have fun, too. There are puzzles and projects, pictures to color, and exercises to do.

ALWAYS REMEMBER The Reason We Play Bridge is FUN

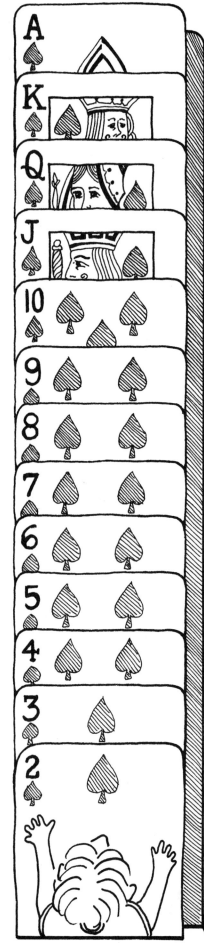

THE DECK

There are (52) cards in the deck.

These 52 cards are divided into 4 groups called SUITS
Here are the 4 suits:

In each suit there are 13 cards.

Here are the 13 cards:
Ace King Queen Jack 10 9 8 7 6 5 4 3 2

The Ace, King, Queen, and Jack are called

HONOR CARDS

They are like a royal family.

The rest of the cards are called

SPOT CARDS

They are covered with suit-shaped spots!
These spots add up to the number on the card.

DO IT! · FIND A DECK OF CARDS.
· SEPARATE THE CARDS INTO SUITS.
· PUT THE CARDS OF EACH SUIT IN ORDER — ACE FIRST, THEN KING, AND SO ON, TO THE 2. NOW YOU SEE THE CARDS IN ORDER.

RANKING

Just like in the army, where soldiers have
RANKINGS like Major, or General, each card
and each suit has a special RANK.

The ACE is the highest RANKING card in each suit.
The KING is the next highest RANKING card.
The QUEEN is the third highest RANKING card.
The JACK is fourth highest, then 10 9 8 7 6 5 4 3 2
all RANKING by their number, 10 first.

CLUBS are the lowest RANKING suit
DIAMONDS are the 2nd lowest RANKING suit.
HEARTS are the 2nd highest RANKING suit.
SPADES are the HIGHEST
RANKING suit.
CLUBS and DIAMONDS are the
MINOR suits. HEARTS and
SPADES are the MAJOR suits.

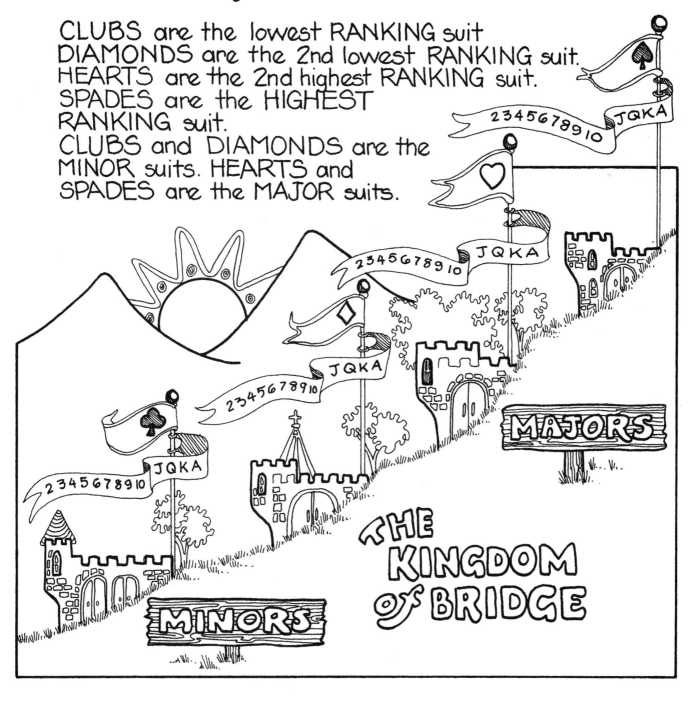

WHAT DO YOU KNOW ?

1. How many cards are there in the deck? _____
2. What are the four suits? _____ _____ _____ _____
3. How many cards are there in each suit? _____
4. What are the cards in each suit? _____ _____ _____ _____
_____ _____ _____ _____ _____ _____ _____ _____ _____

5. What are the honor cards? _____ _____ _____ _____
6. What are the spot cards? _____ _____ _____ _____ _____ _____
_____ _____ _____ _____ _____

7. How many spot cards does that make? _____
8. How many Aces are there in each suit? _____
9. How many Aces are there in the whole deck? _____
   (THINK: how many Aces in each suit, how many suits.)

10. How many tens are there in the whole deck? _____
11. Count the number of ♣'s in the whole deck. _____
12. Can you draw the symbols for each suit?

13. What is the highest ranking suit? _____
14. What is the lowest ranking suit? _____

15. Which are the MINOR suits? _____
16. Which are the MAJOR suits? _____

17. Which is the LOWER ranking suit? ♡ or ♠ _____
18. Which is the HIGHER ranking suit? ♣ or ♡ _____
19. Which is the LOWER ranking suit? ◇ or ♠ _____

20. Circle the highest ranking card
    a. A 3 5 9 7 10   d. 5 3 2 4 6 7
    b. 2 9 8 4 6 7   e. Q 10 9 5 J A
    c. 5 7 10 3 K 2   f. A 8 2 6 9 Q
21. Circle the highest ranking suit.
    a. ♣ ◇ ♠   c. ♣ ◇ ♡
    b. ◇ ♡ ♣   d. ◇ ♣ ♠ ♡

Dealing The Cards

Everyone takes turns dealing the cards. To see who deals first, everyone can pick a card from the deck. The person with the highest card is the dealer. After this, you take turns. The person to the LEFT of the dealer is next.

When we were learning to play bridge, we and our friends would always forget who was dealer. So we found a big green hat for the dealer to wear! This way we never lost track again... until we lost the hat!

Before you deal the cards you have to mix them up, or 'shuffle' them. If you have trouble shuffling, try this easy way. ◇ ◇ ◇ ◇

LIKE THIS

Put all the cards FACE DOWN on the table and just mix them up with your hands. When you have done this enough, gather the cards back into a tidy deck and deal them out.
DEAL ONE CARD AT A TIME.
Start with the person on your left and then deal around the table, giving a card to yourself last.

DEAL ALL OF THE CARDS! Soon there
will be no cards left to deal ~ everyone has **13** cards.

CARDS TOO BIG?

Some kids' hands are too small to hold the cards!

HOW TO MAKE A CARD HOLDER:

You need any small box with a lid like a candy or shoe box. All you do is put the lid on the box and turn it upside down!

Now put your cards in the crack so you can see them!

Decorate your card holder with shiny foil, colored paper, stickers, macaroni, beads, and so on. Now put your name on it.

YOUR VERY OWN CARD HOLDER IS FINISHED!

☆ REMEMBER

THE CARDS YOU HOLD IN YOUR HAND OR YOUR NEW CARD HOLDER ARE **YOUR SECRET.** HOLD YOUR CARDS SO THAT NOBODY CAN SEE WHAT YOUR SECRET IS.

WHIST

Now that you know all
about cards and suits, let's play
a game called **WHIST**. It's very easy.

If you learn this game it will help a lot when
you are playing bridge. Whist was being played
before bridge and was part of the beginning of bridge.

In whist you play with **4** people, but if you don't have
four people, you can still play with two, three, or five. Just
be sure you all have the same number of cards. Put the
extra cards to one side.

In whist, everyone plays one card at a time. The person
to the left of the dealer puts a card face up on the table.
Of course, you keep your cards a secret, until it is time to
play one. Now the rest of your cards are still a secret, right?
The person to the left puts a card on the table, and so on, until
everyone has played one card.

The person who played the **HIGHEST CARD**
wins **ALL OF THEM.**

The winner gets to gather these cards into a little pile
and keep them until the next game. This pile is called

 A TRICK !

The winner just won **A TRICK**, now that was

EASY, HUH?

BUT THERE IS A RULE
TO REMEMBER...

☆☆RULE

EVERYONE MUST FOLLOW SUIT!

This means that if the first person played a spade, then everyone must play a spade. If the first card played was a heart, then everyone must play a heart. You must play a card in the same suit as the first card played.

IT'S A GOOD IDEA

To sort (or arrange) your cards into suits at the beginning, so you don't get mixed up.

If you don't have any cards in the suit played, you have to play another suit.

BUT: this card won't win the TRICK no matter how "BIG" it is. Only if you play the highest card in the right suit, will you win the TRICK.

The first person to play a card is called the LEADER.

The first card played is called the LEAD.

EVERYONE MUST

The person who wins the **TRICK** gets to be the next **LEADER**. Again, EVERYONE has to play the same suit **LED** by the **LEADER**.

When all the cards are played into **TRICKS**, the game is over and the person who has the most tricks is the winner.

The cards which the dealer deals to you are called your

HAND

Each time you play one game or round of whist it is called a **HAND**.

We guess this is because each time you play, you use up all of the cards in your hand.

DO IT YOU CAN PLAY WHIST!

ALL YOU HAVE TO DO IS GO FIND SOME PEOPLE AND PLAY SOME HANDS.

TRUMP

Have you ever played a card game that has WILD CARDS? Sometimes these cards can be Jokers, 2's, or 8's, like in Crazy 8's.
In whist we can have wild cards, too. These are called TRUMP CARDS

In whist, TRUMP CARDS are any card in one certain suit. You can say CLUBS will be TRUMP in the first hand. DIAMONDS will be TRUMP in the second hand. HEARTS will be TRUMP in the third hand, and SPADES will be TRUMP in the fourth hand. Now, for a ᵞSURPRISEᵞ, in the fifth hand there will be NO TRUMP.

TRUMP CARDS are better than any card in any other suit.

BUT you can only play a trump card if you have no more cards in the suit that was led.

IF the lead was diamonds, say, and you have no more diamonds in your hand, you can play a TRUMP CARD and win the trick.

WIN TRUMPS! WITH YAY! RAH! HURRAY!

Even though your TRUMP CARD is not the HIGHEST CARD it still wins the trick.

WHEN can a trump card lose? Only when somebody plays a HIGHER TRUMP CARD than yours, on the trick.

SO: HIGHER TRUMPS BEAT LOWER TRUMPS.

TRUMP!

☆ REMEMBER

NO ONE CAN USE A
TRUMP CARD
UNLESS THEY HAVE
NO MORE CARDS
IN THE SUIT THAT WAS LED.

SOMETIMES
SOMEONE WILL
LEAD TRUMP.
THEN EVERYONE MUST PLAY
A TRUMP,
IF THEY HAVE ONE. OF COURSE,
HIGHEST ONE WINS.

GOOD HANDS

GOOD HANDS WOULD BE ONES
WITH LOTS OF HONOR CARDS
AND LOTS OF
TRUMP CARDS.

WITH A HAND LIKE THAT
YOU COULD WIN
A LOT OF TRICKS,
COULDN'T YOU?

I have
lots of SPADES.
Would it ever be
NEAT
if I could pick
SPADES
as trump...

IN WHIST
YOU CAN'T PICK
TRUMP.

BUT IN BRIDGE, YOU CAN!

WHEN YOU LEARN TO PLAY BRIDGE,
YOU WILL FIND OUT HOW.

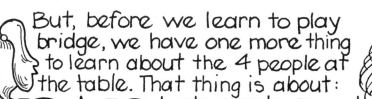

But, before we learn to play bridge, we have one more thing to learn about the 4 people at the table. That thing is about:

PARTNERS

By now, we hope you have played lots and lots of whist!
Play with Mom or Dad, sisters or brothers, schoolmates or playmates, old friends or new friends. The more you play the better you get at following suit and winning tricks and understanding about TRUMP cards.

The next step in learning to play bridge is to play whist with a PARTNER.
There is you and your PARTNER, and you play against someone else and their PARTNER.

YOU and PARTNER are a TEAM!

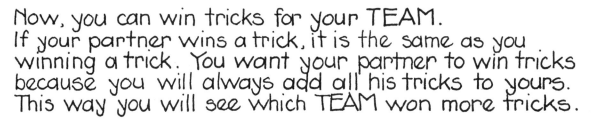

With somebody to help you, you can be twice as good.

Now, you can win tricks for your TEAM.
If your partner wins a trick, it is the same as you winning a trick. You want your partner to win tricks because you will always add all his tricks to yours. This way you will see which TEAM won more tricks.

At the end of each hand you count all the TRICKS your team won, and all the TRICKS which the OPPONENTS won.

THE OPPONENTS

are the two people on the other TEAM.

Your
Partner always sits across
the table from you. The Opponents sit
across the table from each other.

Deal the cards like you do for whist. You will see
that with 4 people, everyone gets 13 cards. Do you
remember from before?

Because each person has 13 cards, there are 13
tricks to be won. This is because everyone will play
one card on each trick.

After everyone has sorted their cards into suits, the
LEADER leads a card. Everyone must follow suit.
If you don't have any cards in the suit led, you may
play a trump card. BUT you don't have to play a
trump. You could just throw away a card from
another suit. The winner of the trick is
either the highest card or the
highest trump card.

Sit at the table,
What do I see?
My wonderful
　　　partner,
Across from me.

And a playing field
One table wide
With each opponent
On either side.

❧ REMEMBER ❧

The tricks that partner wins are added to the tricks that you win for a grand total.
Your PARTNER is on your TEAM!

GOOD IDEA

If your partner has played a high card and no one else has played a higher card or a trump card, then you DON'T HAVE TO BEAT THAT HIGH CARD TO WIN THE TRICK. WHY?

That's right! Because the trick your partner wins is already a trick for your side. You can SAVE your good cards for another trick. If you and your partner both win a trick, it's still only one trick.

example:

If the leader has led a ◇, and your partner has played the ACE of ◇'s, you can play a little ◇ and let his ACE win the trick for your side. Even if you have no ◇'s, YOU DON'T HAVE TO PLAY TRUMP!

FUN PAGE

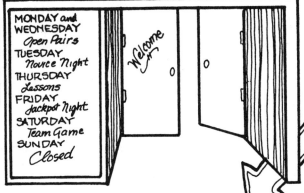

the KOKANEE BRIDGE CLUB

MONDAY and WEDNESDAY
Open Pairs
TUESDAY
Novice Night
THURSDAY
Lessons
FRIDAY
Jackpot Night
SATURDAY
Team Game
SUNDAY
Closed

Welcome

JOHN, BETTY, PAT, and LORI ALL PLAY BRIDGE AT THE KOKANEE BRIDGE CLUB. SEE IF YOU CAN WORK OUT WHO IS LIKELY TO BE AT THE CLUB EACH NIGHT.

Betty is an experienced player. She likes to be John's partner when she can. Betty goes out 3 times a week, but doesn't like team games.

John won last week's jackpot! When he's not giving lessons, John tries to play one open pairs and one team game. John works Monday and Sunday nights.

Pat is a promising novice. He'll play anytime, but doesn't take lessons. He often has trouble finding a team.

Lori is a novice who takes lessons. She doesn't like open pairs. Sometimes she plays with Pat and loves to play in the team events.

TIME PUZZLE

If 8 people played 26 hands in 3 hours. How long would it take 4 people?

HOW MANY KIDS!?

Two of the Brown kids play bridge and three play baseball. What is the smallest possible number of Brown children?

ODD PICTURE

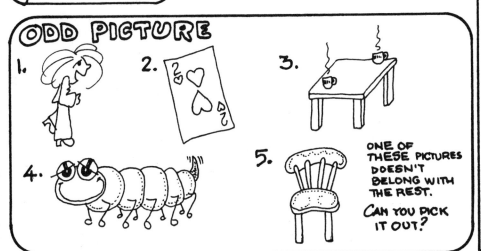

1.
2.
3.
4.
5.

ONE OF THESE PICTURES DOESN'T BELONG WITH THE REST.

CAN YOU PICK IT OUT?

think & remember

You and your partner are a TEAM.
If partner plays a card before you,
  you can usually tell what card to play
  so that either you or partner can win
  the trick, if possible.
    Sometimes you can **HELP** partner, too!
You might know that partner has no ◇'s, so when
you get to be leader, you can lead a little ◇ for
partner to play a trump on.

HISTORY

After people had learned to play
  whist many, many years ago, they
  began to work on the game
    to make it better and more
    fun.
  Remember how we thought it
    would be nice to be able to
    pick our longest suit to be
    trump?
  Well, so did the people
    working on different kinds of
  games of whist. They came up
  with a game called bridge.
Of course, they kept trying to improve bridge, too, until
finally a man named Harold Vanderbilt invented a game
of bridge, and a way of scoring, called CONTRACT BRIDGE.

Mr. Vanderbilt and his friends were on an ocean cruise
at the time, and all helped perfect this new game.
It was such a good game that today, about sixty years
later, we still play bridge in much the same way.

now introducing BRIDGE

Bridge is a lot like whist. You play with 4 people, 2 sets of partners.

Some of you who are part of a big family will find it easier to get 3 other kids to play.

If you don't have a big family, you will need to find some other kids who want to learn the game.

IT'S A GOOD IDEA

Why not start your own Bridge Club?

You could get together once a week (or more!) and play. It's alright if there's more than 4 kids, because you can take turns. The kids not playing can watch. When we play, we usually play 4 hands, and then one player changes places with someone who was watching.

Of course, if there's 4 extra people, they can get a deck of cards, and PLAY BRIDGE!

People who are watching a game of bridge are called

kibitzers

KIBITZERS are good to have around because they can get more juice, change the record, make the popcorn, tell jokes, keep the score, and do many other things.

You could make up a list like this for your club:

OUR BRIDGE CLUB

NAME OF CLUB: _ _ _ _ _ _ _ _ _ _ _ _ _ _

CLUB SITE: _ _ _ _ _ _ _ _ _ _ _ _ _ _

CLUB DAYS: _ _ _ _ _ _ _ _ _ _ _ _ _ _

CLUB MEMBERS: PHONE NUMBER:

_____   _____
_____   _____
_____   _____
_____   _____
_____   _____
_____   _____
_____   _____
_____   _____

CLUB DUTIES:

SECRETARY : KEEPS RECORDS. LOOKS AFTER CARDS.

TREASURER: KEEPS TRACK OF CLUB MONEY.

HOSPITALITY: MAKES SURE THERE ARE SNACKS AND DRINKS

MEMBERSHIP SECRETARY: MAKES SURE EVERYONE KNOWS ABOUT MEETINGS KEEPS TRACK OF MEMBERS

BRIDGE

1. THE DEAL
2. THE BIDDING
3. THE PLAY
4. THE SCORE

Number 1, the Deal, you already know from playing whist. Number 3, play, you're already used to, also from whist.

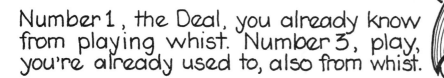

THE BIDDING

The bidding starts after you deal all the cards.
Each one of the 4 people will have 13 cards.
As in whist, sort your hand into suits.
Remember that there are 13 tricks to be won, because each player puts one card on each trick.

What you will be doing in the bidding is trying to pick a trump suit. Also you will promise to win a certain number of tricks, if you and your partner get to have one of your suits as trump.

What about your OPPONENTS?

They will also be trying to pick what is trump.
The TEAM that promises to take the most tricks in the highest ranking suit, wins the bidding.
When the bidding is over, the team that won the bidding plays the hand with their suit as trump. Or, sometimes with nothing as trump.

THERE'S MORE TO LEARN ABOUT BIDDING

▷ ▷ ▷ ▷ ▷ ▷ ▷ ▷ ▷ ▷ ▷ ▷ ▷ ▷ ▷ ▷ ▷

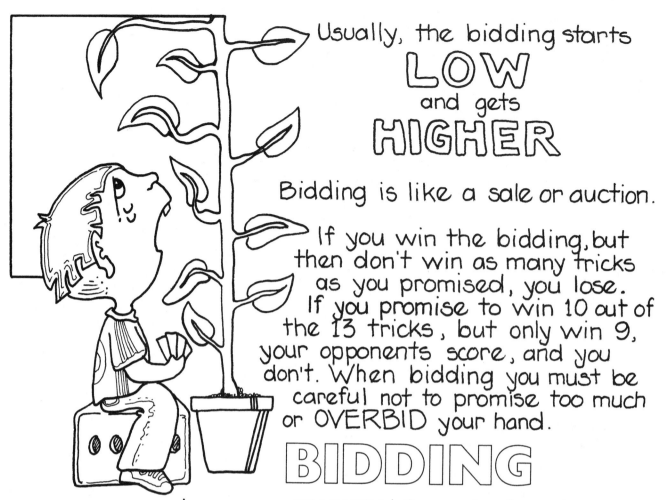

Usually, the bidding starts LOW and gets HIGHER

Bidding is like a sale or auction.

If you win the bidding, but then don't win as many tricks as you promised, you lose. If you promise to win 10 out of the 13 tricks, but only win 9, your opponents score, and you don't. When bidding you must be careful not to promise too much or OVERBID your hand.

BIDDING

is a very EXCITING part of bridge.

Bidding is like a new LANGUAGE, only easier to learn, and there's no spelling, OK?

In the bidding you will be able to tell partner things about your hand. At the same time, you will be hearing things about partner's hand.

Through bidding, you will be able to find out how many tricks your Team might win and what should be trump. Or, you might find out that there should be No Trump. Often, you'll discover that the Opponents are doing a lot of bidding. You will be able to hear what they are telling each other about their hands.

By the time the bidding is over, everyone will have some idea about what everyone's hand is like! This will help when you are playing the hand.

THE SCORE

BRIDGE HAS A SPECIAL WAY OF SCORING

The object of bridge as in many other games is to score more points than your opponents.

If you win all the tricks you bid, you get a GOOD, or PLUS score.

If you don't win all the tricks you bid, you get a BAD, or MINUS score.

Of course, if the opponents win all the tricks they bid, they will get a PLUS score, which is a minus score for you. If they don't win all the tricks, they will be minus, you will be plus.

HERE IS WHAT A SCORESHEET LOOKS LIKE:

their team

our team

WE THEY

YOUR PLUS SCORE GOES HERE

YOUR MINUS SCORE GOES HERE

When kids are learning to play bridge, they sometimes find scoring to be the hardest part. They don't like all the adding and subtracting. It can be a lot like MATH and school.

Some kids don't like math very much and maybe you don't either.

Just in case, in the back of this book there is a page with every possible score. You can use this page and we won't bore you with the math.

For those of you who do want to learn how to score, we have put a page at the back of the book to teach you how it is done.

After you have played as many hands as you want, you add up the scores on each side.

The team with the bigger score

≋WINS≋

BRIDGE ART

BRIDGE ART IS WHAT WE CALL THE WAY WE WRITE ABOUT BRIDGE ON PAPER.

Instead of writing CLUBS, DIAMONDS, HEARTS, and SPADES, we draw: ♣ ◇ ♡ ♤

Instead of drawing a bridge table like [drawing] OR [drawing] we draw =[square]

We draw the table as if we were looking down on it.

Instead of drawing bridge players, and naming them YOU, OPENER, THE GUY ON YOUR LEFT, or THE GIRL WITH THE RIBBON, we just call them NORTH, EAST, SOUTH and WEST.

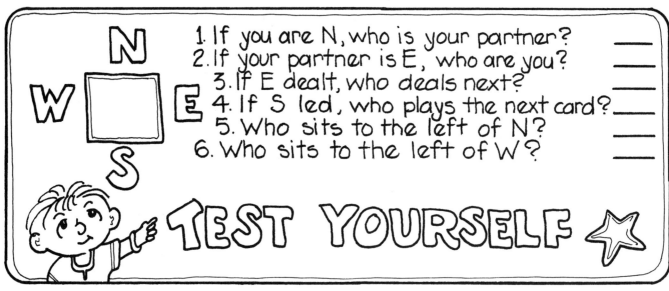

N
W □ E
S

1. If you are N, who is your partner? _____
2. If your partner is E, who are you? _____
3. If E dealt, who deals next? _____
4. If S led, who plays the next card? _____
5. Who sits to the left of N? _____
6. Who sits to the left of W? _____

TEST YOURSELF ★

Instead of drawing out all of the cards,

— like this

Everytime we want to write down a hand we draw like this:

the cards

The spades are always on top, then the hearts, then the diamonds, and then clubs on the bottom.

♠ AKQJ
♡ J1032
♢ AKQ
♣ AK

(by the way, this is a good hand, isn't it!)

the suits

Sometimes, everything is drawn in one picture,　like this

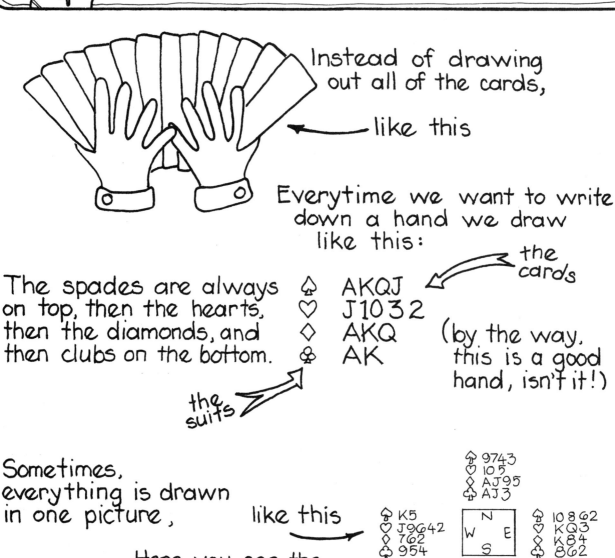

♠ 9743
♡ 105
♢ AJ95
♣ AJ3

♠ K5
♡ J9642
♢ 762
♣ 954

N
W E
S

♠ 10862
♡ KQ3
♢ K84
♣ 862

♠ AQJ
♡ A87
♢ Q103
♣ KQ107

Here you see the table, the people, and all the hands the people hold. You can see the whole deck.

34

HOW GOOD IS YOUR HAND?

When you pick up your hand, and sort it into suits, what would you like to see?

RIGHT! You would like to see lots and lots of HONOR cards. With lots of honor cards you know you are going to win some tricks.

> From now on, we are going to call these honor cards (AKQJ) *HIGH CARDS*

> There once was a man named MILTON WORK who invented a way to find out exactly how good your hand is. He decided that each honor card would be worth a certain number of points. We call these points: *HIGH CARD POINTS*

Sometimes we just write, or say H C P
Here is what they are worth:
ACE = 4 H C P   KING = 3 H C P
QUEEN = 2 H C P
JACK = 1 H C P

Counting your points
    Is easy you see
Aces are worth four
    Kings are worth three
Queens count for two
    Jacks count for one
Add them all up
    And your first job is done!

THE DECK

There are 4 Aces in the deck	♠A	4	H C P
	♥A	4	H C P
	♦A	4	H C P
	♣A	4	H C P
There are 4 Kings in the deck	♠K	3	H C P
	♥K	3	H C P
	♦K	3	H C P
	♣K	3	H C P
There are 4 Queens in the deck	♠Q	2	H C P
	♥Q	2	H C P
	♦Q	2	H C P
	♣Q	2	H C P
There are 4 Jacks in the deck	♠J	1	H C P
	♥J	1	H C P
	♦J	1	H C P
	♣J	1	H C P

HOW MANY HIGH CARD POINTS
(H C P) ARE IN THE WHOLE
DECK?   ADD THEM UP ⟶

THERE ARE
40 HIGH CARD POINTS
IN THE WHOLE DECK

There are 10 HCP in each suit!

♠ A(4) K(3) Q(2) J(1) = 10
♡ A(4) K(3) Q(2) J(1) = 10
♢ A(4) K(3) Q(2) J(1) = 10
♣ A(4) K(3) Q(2) J(1) = 10

IN THE WHOLE DECK   40 HCP

If you have lots of
HIGH CARD POINTS
you have a

GOOD HAND

When you are bidding in bridge you always count your points and add them to what points partner has.

IN THE BIDDING

You will find out how many points partner has.

WHEN YOU GET A NEW HAND

1. SORT INTO SUITS

2. COUNT YOUR POINTS

count your hand

Here are some exercises to help you practice COUNTING YOUR HAND. You will notice that these hands are written as we described in BRIDGE ART.

1. ♠ KQ _____
    ♡ Q _____
    ♢ A 10 7 6 5 _____
    ♣ KJ 9 6 5 _____
    TOTAL HCP _____

2. ♠ AK 6 _____
    ♡ AK 10 3 _____
    ♢ Q 3 2 _____
    ♣ 9 4 3 _____
    TOTAL HCP _____

3. ♠ Q 8 7 2 _____
    ♡ 6 5 2 _____
    ♢ AK 6 _____
    ♣ J 10 5 _____
    TOTAL HCP _____

4. ♠ AQJ 9 8 7 _____
    ♡ K 10 _____
    ♢ 8 2 _____
    ♣ AK 3 _____
    TOTAL HCP _____

5. ♠ 6 3 2 _____
    ♡ AJ 7 6 _____
    ♢ 4 3 _____
    ♣ J 10 9 6 _____
    TOTAL HCP _____

6. ♠ AKQJ _____
    ♡ Q 10 4 _____
    ♢ AK 6 2 _____
    ♣ J 10 _____
    TOTAL HCP _____

7. How many HCP in the whole deck?

8. How many HCP in one suit?

9. How many HCP are each of the following worth?

    a. A _____   d. J _____   g. AK _____
    b. K _____   e. QJ _____   h. AJ _____
    c. Q _____   f. AQ _____   i. KQ _____

10. Which of the hands numbered 1 to 6 above is the best hand? _____

11. Which of the hands 1 to 6 is the worst? _____

THE BIDDING

Let's talk some more about bidding.

When you are bidding, you are saying you are going to take a certain number of tricks if your suit is trump.

When bridge was being worked on years ago, a rule was borrowed from a kind of whist. This was that the first six tricks won by one side or the other were called

THE BOOK

They called it 'the book' because those six tricks looked like a book when they were piled together.

In bridge, we use this 'book' in bidding. If we had to bid for the 13 tricks that there are, it would take a long time. Since the book of 6 tricks is 1 less than half of 13 tricks, we do not use it in the bidding. When you are bidding you are saying you will win

THE BOOK + The number of tricks you bid.

If you bid 1♣ you are saying you will win
   6 Tricks + 1 more if Clubs are trump.

If you bid 2♣ you are saying you will win
   6 Tricks + 2 more if Clubs are trump.

IN BIDDING YOU ARE ALWAYS SAYING
HOW MANY MORE TRICKS YOU WILL WIN
AFTER YOU HAVE WON 6 TRICKS
OR THE BOOK.

up the bidding ladder

7NT
7♣
7♡
7♢
7♣
6NT
6♣
6♡
6♢
6♣
5NT
5♣
5♡
5♢
5♣
4NT
4♣
4♡
4♢
4♣
3NT
3♣
3♡
3♢
3♣
2NT
2♣
2♡
2♢
2♣
1NT
1♣
1♡
1♢
1♣

Think of bidding as climbing a ladder.

EACH BID MUST BE HIGHER THAN THE LAST!

☆ THE DEALER STARTS THE BIDDING
Then the person to the left of the dealer can bid next. And so on to each person to the left, back to the dealer. The dealer can bid again if he wants, then 'round and 'round the bidding goes, always to the left.

☆ YOU DON'T HAVE TO BID!
If you don't want to bid you just say

PASS!

☆ THREE PASSES IN A ROW
after the bidding has started means

THE BIDDING IS OVER!

THE TEAM which made THE LAST BID before the bidding went PASS·PASS·PASS WINS THE BIDDING. They have promised to win six tricks plus as many more as they bid. They get to have their suit as trump.

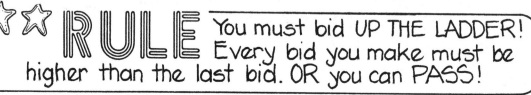

☆☆ RULE You must bid UP THE LADDER! Every bid you make must be higher than the last bid. OR you can PASS!

Look At The Ladder

1♣ is the lowest bid that can be made.
7NT is the highest bid that can be made.
There are 35 possible bids - COUNT THEM.
1◇ is one bid higher than 1♣.
4NT is one bid lower than 5♣.
2♡ is one bid higher than 2◇.

LOOKING AT THE BIDDING LADDER
fill in the missing bids

1. 3NT _____ 5♣
2. 2♠ _____ 3NT
3. 1♡ _____ 2NT
4. 4♡ _____ 6♡
5. 5♣ _____ 6◇
6. 1NT _____ 3NT

7. How many ONE BIDS are there? _____
   What are they? _____

8. How many THREE BIDS are there? _____
   What are they? _____

remember

CLUBS COME FIRST, THEN
DIAMONDS, THEN HEARTS,
THEN SPADES, THEN NT
(NO TRUMP). Spades are the highest
ranking suit. Clubs are the lowest.

41

HERE ARE ALL THE BIDS

CAN YOU FILL IN WHAT EACH BID SAYS?

6 TRICKS + 7 MORE (13 TRICKS) IF NOTHING IS TRUMP
6 TRICKS + _ MORE (_ TRICKS) IF _____ IS TRUMP
_ TRICKS + _ MORE (_ TRICKS) IF _____ IS TRUMP

7NT
7♠
7♡
7♢
7♣
6NT
6♠
6♡
6♢
6♣
5NT
5♠
5♡
5♢
5♣
4NT
4♠
4♡
4♢
4♣
3NT
3♠
3♡
3♢
3♣
2NT
2♠
2♡
2♢
2♣
1NT
1♠
1♡
1♢
1♣

WHEW!

WHAT DO YOU KNOW ?

1. What is THE BOOK ?

2. If you bid the following how many tricks are you saying your team can win ?
   a. 4NT _6_ TRICKS + _4_ MORE WITH _NOTHING_ AS TRUMP.
   b. 2♠ ___ ___ ___
   c. 1NT ___ ___ ___
   d. 3♣ ___ ___ ___
   e. 2◇ ___ ___ ___
   f. 3♡ ___ ___ ___
   g. 5♠ ___ ___ ___
   h. 4◇ ___ ___ ___
   i. 6♡ ___ ___ ___
   j. 3◇ ___ ___ ___
   k. 2NT ___ ___ ___
   l. 7♡ ___ ___ ___
   m. 5♣ ___ ___ ___
   n. 3NT ___ ___ ___
   o. 4♡ ___ ___ ___
   p. 2◇ ___ ___ ___
   q. 1NT ___ ___ ___
   r. 3♠ ___ ___ ___
   s. 5NT ___ ___ ___
   t. 6♡ ___ ___ ___

3. If you bid the following, how many tricks altogether are you saying you will win ?
   a. 3NT ___ tricks   e. 1NT ___ tricks
   b. 4♡ ___ tricks   f. 2♡ ___ tricks
   c. 5◇ ___ tricks   g. 5◇ ___ tricks
   d. 6♠ ___ tricks   h. 4♠ ___ tricks

THINK! FOR THE HARD THINKERS

4. If you bid the following how many tricks can you LOSE but still win the number that you bid? (Hint: Subtract the number you'll win from 13, right ?)
   a. 3NT___   b. 4♡___   c. 5◇___   d. 7NT___

LEVELS

IT MIGHT HELP YOU TO THINK
OF ALL THE BIDS
AS IF
THEY WERE ON
DIFFERENT LEVELS.

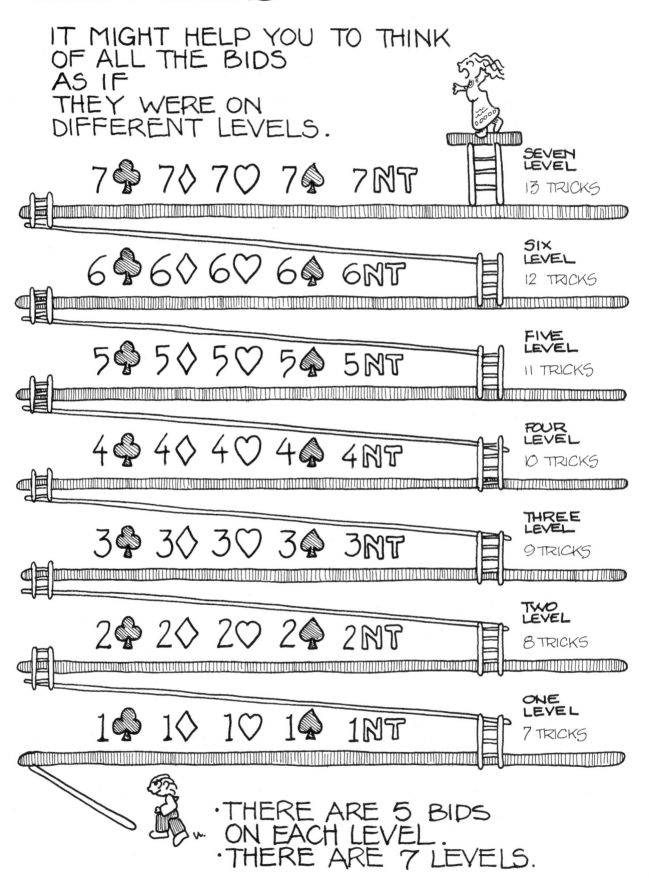

7♣ 7◇ 7♡ 7♠ 7NT — SEVEN LEVEL — 13 TRICKS

6♣ 6◇ 6♡ 6♠ 6NT — SIX LEVEL — 12 TRICKS

5♣ 5◇ 5♡ 5♠ 5NT — FIVE LEVEL — 11 TRICKS

4♣ 4◇ 4♡ 4♠ 4NT — FOUR LEVEL — 10 TRICKS

3♣ 3◇ 3♡ 3♠ 3NT — THREE LEVEL — 9 TRICKS

2♣ 2◇ 2♡ 2♠ 2NT — TWO LEVEL — 8 TRICKS

1♣ 1◇ 1♡ 1♠ 1NT — ONE LEVEL — 7 TRICKS

• THERE ARE 5 BIDS ON EACH LEVEL.
• THERE ARE 7 LEVELS.

44

THE CONTRACT

The highest bid made before you hear PASS·PASS·PASS is called THE CONTRACT.

All of the bidding up to the highest bid and 3 passes is called THE AUCTION.

If the highest bid made in THE AUCTION was 2♠, then THE CONTRACT is 2♠. If the highest bid made was 3NT, then THE CONTRACT is 3NT.

Whichever team bid the last or highest bid in the auction WINS the bidding and must play the contract. They must win 6 tricks plus however many more they promised in bidding to make their contract.

THE CONTRACT tells: 1. How many tricks must be won. 2. If there is trump, or no trump. 3. What suit is trump.

When all the cards have been played, the hand is over. If you won enough tricks for your contract you will get a PLUS SCORE.

If you didn't make your contract, you get a MINUS score, or rather, they get a PLUS SCORE.

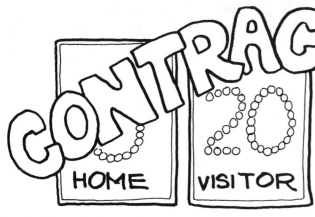 **CONTRACT**

DIFFERENT CONTRACTS SCORE DIFFERENT AMOUNTS OF POINTS.

A MINOR SUIT CONTRACT
♣ ♦ SCORES THE LEAST AMOUNT OF POINTS

A MAJOR SUIT CONTRACT
♡ ♠ SCORES MORE THAN A MINOR SUIT

A NO TRUMP CONTRACT
NT SCORES THE LARGEST AMOUNT OF POINTS

When people were working on making the game better and better, they decided that there would be a

BONUS SCORE

If you bid to a high level, and won all the tricks you promised, you would be rewarded. They decided to award the BONUS SCORE if you bid to a contract called a

GAME CONTRACT
❋❋❋❋❋❋❋❋❋❋❋❋❋❋

If you bid and make a GAME CONTRACT you get hundreds of extra points.

THE GAME CONTRACTS ARE :

3NT 4♡ 4♠ 5♣ 5♦

GAME CONTRACTS

3NT

If you bid up to 3NT and you make ⑨ tricks (6 + 3 more) you would get a BONUS SCORE.

4♥ 4♠

If you bid up to 4♥ or 4♠ and you make ⑩ tricks (6 + 4 more) you would get a BONUS SCORE because you made a MAJOR SUIT GAME.

5♣ 5♦

If you bid up to 5♣ or 5♦ and you won ⑪ tricks (6 + 5 more) you would get a BONUS SCORE because you made a MINOR SUIT GAME. ← LOOK

You need to win ⑪ tricks to make a game in the MINOR SUITS.
You need to win ⑩ tricks to make a game in the MAJOR SUITS.
You need to win ONLY ⑨ tricks to make a game in NO TRUMP.

This has made the MINOR SUITS less popular in Bridge. If you can play a NO TRUMP contract then you will want to bid up to 3NT (9 tricks) if you can, to get your BONUS. If you don't have the kind of hand to play in NO TRUMP, then you would pick a MAJOR SUIT (10 tricks) if you could.

If you are in the following contracts, how many tricks can you LOSE and still win enough tricks to make your contract?

1NT _____

3♥ _____

7♠ _____

4♣ _____

5♦ _____

2♥ _____

6♣ _____

4♥ _____

1♠ _____

IAN'S partner won this many tricks.

· How many tricks did IAN'S opponents win? _____
· How many tricks did IAN'S opponents lose? _____
· How many tricks did IAN win? _____
· Did IAN'S opponents make their contract of 2NT? _____

MATCH the number of tricks with the right contract

12 TRICKS   4♥
9 TRICKS   7NT
10 TRICKS   3NT
11 TRICKS   2♠
7 TRICKS   5♦
8 TRICKS   6♣
13 TRICKS   1NT

MR. BROWN is making a face. But we know that bridge is more fun if we are happy. MRS. BROWN knows the secret. Turn the page upsidedown!

☆ REMEMBER

The MINOR SUIT GAME needs the MOST tricks and scores the LEAST points. **11 TRICKS**

The MAJOR SUIT GAME needs LESS tricks and scores MORE points. **10 TRICKS**

The NO TRUMP GAME needs the LEAST tricks and often scores the MOST points. **9 TRICKS**

☆ ☆ RULE

YOU ONLY GET YOUR GAME BONUS IF YOU BID THE GAME.

If your contract is 2♤ and you win 10 tricks (6 † 4 more) you DON'T get your BONUS.
If your contract is 4♤ (6 † 4 more, spades as trumps) and you win 10 tricks (6 + 4 more) you DO get your BONUS SCORE.

You must bid at least
3NT 4♡ 4♤ 5♧ or 5◇
and make the tricks you bid
in order to get your BONUS SCORE.

If you don't bid up to game, and play a contract below game, this is called a PARTIAL

You only get PART of the score you would have got if you had BID GAME.

WHAT DO YOU KNOW ?

1. What is THE CONTRACT ? _____ _____

2. Which kind of CONTRACT scores the most points? _____

3. Which kind of CONTRACT scores the least points? _____

4. Why are GAME CONTRACTS special ? _____ _____

5. What is GAME in NT ? _____ _____

6. How many tricks do you need to win to make GAME in NT? _____ _____

7. How many tricks do you need to win to make GAMES in the MAJOR SUITS ? _____ _____

8. How many tricks do you need to win to make GAMES in the MINOR SUITS ? _____ _____

9. What are GAMES in the MAJORS ? _____ _____

10. What are GAMES in the MINORS ? _____ _____

11. What is the RULE about GAME CONTRACTS? _____ _____

12. Circle the GAME CONTRACTS.

4♡   3♣   5♣   1♠   2♡   3NT
1NT   4♣   4♠   2NT   3♡   5◊   4◊   1♡

13. Which contract needs more tricks?
   a. 4♡ or 5◊   _____
   b. 3♣ or 4♠   _____
   c. 1NT or 2♡   _____
   d. 3NT or 5♣   _____
   e. 4♡ or 6◊   _____
   f. 3♡ or 3NT   _____

50

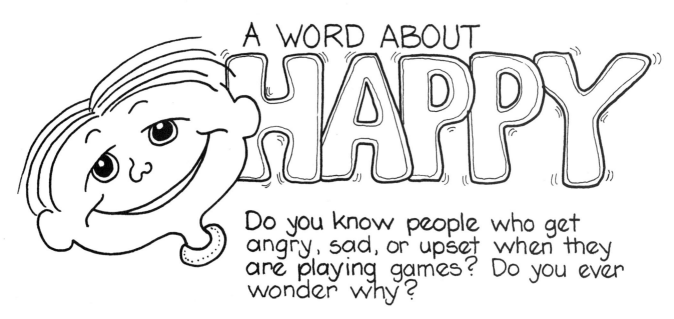

A WORD ABOUT HAPPY

Do you know people who get angry, sad, or upset when they are playing games? Do you ever wonder why?

A lot of times it is because they think that if they don't get angry with themselves, they won't try harder. They think that if they don't get upset, it means they don't care!

BUT **WE** KNOW YOU CAN BE **HAPPY** AND STILL TRY HARDER.

YOU CAN BE **HAPPY** AND CARE!

Happy people can be smart people and happy people **FEEL GOOD!**

AND You don't have to get angry with your partner either! Your partner wants to learn to play bridge, too! If he makes a mistake, you can still be happy. You know he will try harder next time.

BRIDGE IS FUN!

Even if you are the most serious bridge player in the whole world you can still have fun and be happy!

RULE You smile at one
Who smiles at you
And then one smile makes two ...

51

THERE'S ONE THING LEFT TO TELL YOU ABOUT THE SCORE

Because it gets harder and harder for you to take tricks as you bid higher and higher, there is an EXTRA SPECIAL BONUS SCORE given to you if you bid all the way up to the **6 LEVEL** or the **7 LEVEL**.

➡ 6♣ 6♦ 6♡ 6♠ 6NT contracts are called **SMALL SLAMS** and to make a SMALL SLAM you must win 12 tricks.

➡ 7♣ 7♦ 7♡ 7♠ 7NT contracts are called **GRAND SLAMS** and to make a GRAND SLAM you must win 13 tricks. Let's see what we know – bidding up to a small slam means taking all but 1 trick. Bidding up to a grand slam means taking all of the tricks. Of course you and your partner will need to have pretty good hands to be able to bid all the way up into **THE SLAM ZONE.**

DECLARER AND DUMMY

We already know that when the bidding is over, one team or the other has won THE CONTRACT.

The team which has won THE CONTRACT is the team who has promised to take the larger number of tricks.

One person on this team will be DECLARER and one person will be DUMMY.

DECLARER IS THE FIRST PERSON ON THE TEAM TO BID THE TRUMP SUIT OR NO TRUMP. THE OTHER PERSON IS DUMMY.

Let's say that the East - West team has won the bidding of the hand with a bid of 4♠. Now E-W must remember who bid ♠ first. If E bid ♠ first, then E is declarer. If W bid ♠ first, then W is declarer.

If the contract is 3NT and W bid some number of NT first, early in the bidding, it doesn't matter who bid 3NT because W will be the DECLARER.

When W is the declarer, E is the DUMMY.
When E is the declarer, W is the DUMMY.
The same is true for North- South, (N-S)

The title DECLARER goes to the team that named the final CONTRACT, and to the player of that team who first bid the contract trump suit, or no trump.

DUMMY
IS DECLARER'S PARTNER.

AFTER THE OPENING LEAD, DUMMY PUTS HIS HAND DOWN ON THE TABLE FOR EVERYONE TO SEE.

This hand is called THE DUMMY, too. Declarer now gets to play cards from DUMMY as well as from his hand.

The LEADER leads a card, then declarer asks partner to play a card from dummy, then the leader's partner plays a card, and last of all DECLARER plays a card.

The cards are played in the same order as in WHIST. Whoever wins a trick makes the next LEAD, and everybody plays in turn TO THE LEFT. Each time it is DUMMY'S TURN to PLAY or LEAD, DECLARER gets to choose what card DUMMY must play.
What is really neat about this is that DECLARER can see both hands and can choose whether to try to win the trick with a card from hand or a card from dummy.
If DECLARER wins a trick in dummy, the
54 LEAD must come from dummy.

DUMMY IS LAID DOWN IN SUITS.

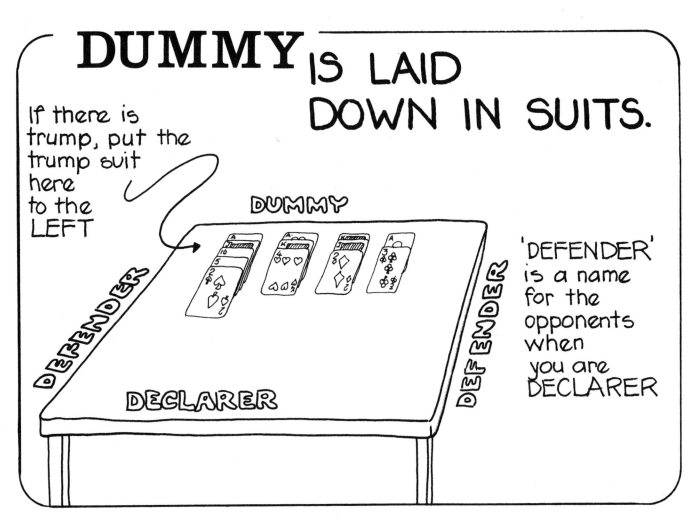

If there is trump, put the trump suit here to the LEFT

DUMMY

DEFENDER

DECLARER

DEFENDER

'DEFENDER' is a name for the opponents when you are DECLARER

TRICKS ARE LAID DOWN LIKE THIS.

These are TRICKS that you and your partner have won.

THE DEFENDERS

The DEFENDERS are the two players who did not win the contract.
The DEFENDERS work together to try to make sure that the declarer will not win all of the tricks needed to make the contract.
If declarer does not win all the tricks that are needed to make the contract, then declarer's team

GOES DOWN

If declarer makes one fewer trick declarer's team is DOWN ONE.
If declarer wins two fewer tricks declarer's team is DOWN TWO.

THE DEFENDERS ARE TRYING TO MAKE DECLARER GO DOWN.

IF DECLARER GOES DOWN IN THE CONTRACT THE DEFENDERS WILL GET A PLUS SCORE.

SAME CARDS

JERRY, SUE, AMBER and BETH ALL THINK THEY HAVE THE SAME HAND AS JACK. WHO IS RIGHT?

JERRY'S HAND

♠ AK103
♡ QJ7
♦ A2
♣ J982

SUE'S HAND

♠ AK103
♡ QJ32
♦ A2
♣ J08

BETH'S HAND

♠ AK103
♡ QJ3
♦ A4
♣ J982

AMBER'S HAND

♠ AK103
♡ QJ3
♦ A2
♣ J982

FIND 'A' WORD

CIRCLE THE WORDS BELOW AS THEY ARE FOUND IN THE PUZZLE. THE WORDS COULD RUN IN ANY DIRECTION...

```
C L U B S R E D N A V O
S R E Z T I B I K A A A
D Z W I N R M P N R N W
I S P B H L I D P B D H
A P M R V E Z C M T E P
M A I I S A A K U U R A
O R R D P D N R R   B U
N T B G I M F A T Z I S
D R Z E K A T N E S L H
S U I T K H M K D B T E
R E N T R A P O S I S L
W H I S T R U P A K B L
W L S L N M A N C D P O
K H C A R D S I A L A T
R W I N E D R S V R U
B R I S D T S M I L E B
```

- BRIDGE
- CARDS
- ~~CLUBS~~
- DIAMONDS
- HEARTS
- KIBITZERS
- LEAD
- PARTNER
- RANK
- SPADES
- SUIT
- TRICKS
- TRUMP
- VANDERBILT
- WHIST

WHO WON?

CAN YOU TELL WHO WON EACH OF THE TRICKS BELOW? CIRCLE WHETHER IT WAS NORTH, SOUTH, EAST OR WEST......

J♡
A♡ [ ] 9♡
2♡
NOTHING TRUMP
N E S (W)

A♣
K♣ [ ] 3♣
2♣
SPADES ARE TRUMP
N E S W

9♦
10♦ [ ] J♦
2♦
HEARTS ARE TRUMP
N E S W

K♣
9♣ [ ] J♣
4♣
NOTHING TRUMP
N E S W

A♣
J♡ [ ] 2♡
4♦
DIAMONDS ARE TRUMP
N E S W

3♡
4♡ [ ] 9♡
5♡
NOTHING TRUMP
N E S W

K♡
Q♡ [ ] 3♣
2♡
CLUBS ARE TRUMP
N E S W

10♣
J♣ [ ] A♣
4♣
NOTHING TRUMP
N E S W

ARE:

To Pick a Trump Suit
Or
Decide to Play No Trump

To Find Out
What Contract to Play
• how high do we bid?
• do we bid a game?

13 is an important number in bridge.
There are 13 cards in each suit.
There are 13 cards in each hand.
IT'S A GOOD IDEA FOR YOU TO
BE VERY FAMILIAR WITH 13

 YOU CAN'T DIVIDE 13 INTO 2 EQUAL GROUPS.

 YOU CAN'T DIVIDE 13 INTO 4 EQUAL GROUPS

 THE 13 CARDS IN ONE SUIT CAN BE DIVIDED
BETWEEN HANDS IN MANY WAYS.

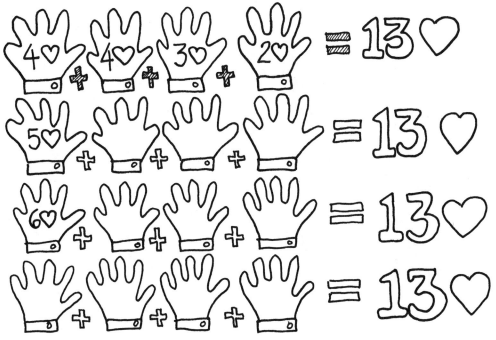

Can you fill in the hands above
differently than the one shown?

THE FIT

HOW DO YOU CHOOSE THE TRUMP SUIT?

You know that you can choose the trump suit by bidding, but how would you know which suit would be best as trump?

If you have a lot of cards in one suit, you should pick it to be trump. Or if partner has lots of cards in a suit, you should pick that as trump.

REMEMBER: If you and partner win the contract, both hands can be used to win tricks. One is DECLARER, one is DUMMY.
The two hands work TOGETHER.

Even if you don't have a long suit and partner doesn't have a long suit, when your hand and partner's hand both have cards in the same suit, you can choose that suit as trump.

☆☆☆ RULE   YOUR TEAM NEEDS AT LEAST 8 CARDS IN ONE SUIT TO PICK IT AS TRUMP.

There are only **13** cards in one suit. If your team has **8** of these you have **3** more than the opponent's **5** cards.

13 CARDS

If you want to pick a trump suit, pick a suit which has

8 or more cards.

YOU WANT TO HAVE AT LEAST THREE MORE TRUMP IN YOUR TWO HANDS than in your OPPONENTS' HANDS.

13 FISH

8 CARDS

You don't have to have all these cards in one hand. They can be shared with partner's hand.

13 STARS

If the number of cards in one suit in your hand

PLUS

the number of cards in the same suit in your partner's hand ADDS UP TO 8 OR MORE THEN YOU AND YOUR PARTNER HAVE

A FIT.

A FIT is 8 CARDS OR MORE
IN ONE SUIT BETWEEN YOUR HAND AND YOUR PARTNER'S HAND.

KINDS OF FITS

THE BEST KIND OF FIT IS ONE WHERE THE CARDS IN A SUIT ARE SHARED EQUALLY BETWEEN TWO HANDS.

4-4 FIT

The 4-4 FIT is where partner has 4 cards in a suit and you have 4 cards in the same suit.

5-3 FIT

The 5-3 FIT is where one of you has 5 cards and the other has 3 cards in the same suit.

ANOTHER KIND OF FIT IS WHERE ONE HAND HAS LOTS OF CARDS IN ONE SUIT, BUT THE OTHER HAND ONLY HAS 2 OR 1 IN THE SUIT.

6-2 FIT

The 6-2 FIT is where one hand has 6 cards and the other has 2 cards in the same suit.

7-1 FIT

The 7-1 FIT is where one hand has 7 cards and the other has 1 card in the same suit.

THESE ARE ALL 8-CARD FITS.

OF COURSE YOU WOULD LIKE A 9-, OR 10-, OR 11-CARD FIT BUT MOST OF YOUR FITS WILL BE AROUND 8 CARDS.

WHAT DO YOU KNOW ?

1. How many cards are there in one suit? _____

2. How many cards should you and partner have before you choose that suit as trump? _____

3. Why do you need that many cards? _____
_____

4. What are 4 different kinds of FIT? _____
_____

5. What is the BEST KIND OF FIT? _____
_____

6. In these hands tell us what suit is your best FIT and what kind of FIT it is.

	YOUR HAND	PARTNER'S HAND	
a)	♠AKJ32 ♡2 ♢KQ10 ♣A987	♠Q54 ♡J10987 ♢A92 ♣106	BEST FIT _____ KIND OF FIT _____
b)	♠J102 ♡65 ♢KQJ104 ♣J103	♠AK5 ♡AKJ843 ♢2 ♣AQ6	BEST FIT _____ KIND OF FIT _____
c)	♠6532 ♡QJ109 ♢76 ♣Q98	♠Q4 ♡A872 ♢9832 ♣KJ10	BEST FIT _____ KIND OF FIT _____
d)	♠AJ ♡AKQJ9 ♢KQJ9 ♣76	♠K1087 ♡432 ♢A104 ♣J109	BEST FIT _____ KIND OF FIT _____
e)	♠A854 ♡J5 ♢K72 ♣KQ84	♠63 ♡K43 ♢A65 ♣AJ1097	BEST FIT _____ KIND OF FIT _____

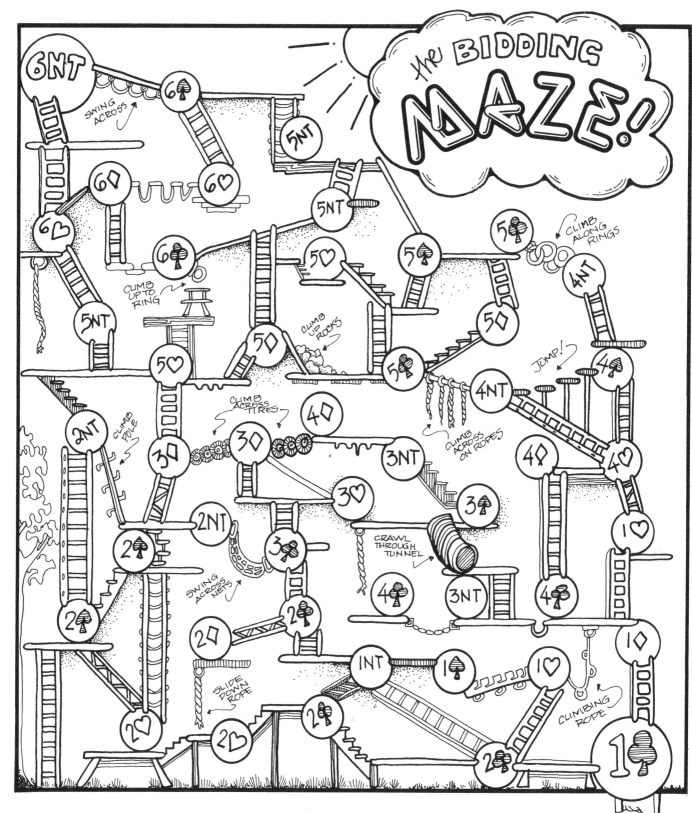

John has found the Adventure Playground of his dreams! He would like to climb to the very top, but he must follow the bids in the correct order.
Can you work out the path through the bidding maze from 1♣ to 6NT?

TEST YOURSELF

1. Why do we play bridge? _____
2. How many cards in the deck? _____
3. How many suits? _____
4. What are the cards? _____
5. What are the suits? _____
6. What are the HONOR CARDS? _____
7. What is the HIGHEST RANKING CARD? _____
8. What is the LOWEST RANKING CARD? _____
9. What is the RANKING of SUITS?

     HIGHEST _____
     NEXT HIGHEST _____
     NEXT _____
     LOWEST _____

10. What are the MAJOR SUITS? _____
11. What are the MINOR SUITS? _____
12. How many Aces in the whole deck? _____
13. How many 3's in the whole deck? _____
14. How many 10's in SPADES? _____
15. In which direction do you deal the cards? _____
16. In BRIDGE, how many cards will each person get? _____
17. What is a trick? _____
_____
18. Who wins a trick? _____
_____
19. Who is the leader in WHIST? _____
_____
20. Who is the leader in BRIDGE? _____
_____
21. What is a hand? _____
_____
22. Wild cards in WHIST and BRIDGE are called? _____
23. What is the RULE about playing to a trick? _____
_____
24. When can you play a TRUMP card? _____
_____
25. When will a TRUMP card LOSE a trick? _____
_____

TEST YOURSELF

26. Are you allowed to lead a TRUMP?
27. What would a GOOD HAND have?
28. If you play whist with a partner you need ___ players.
29. Who is on your team?
30. Who are the OPPONENTS?
31. Where does your partner sit?
32. How many cards does everyone get?
33. How many tricks can be won?
34. What are KIBITZERS?

35. What are the 4 parts of BRIDGE?

36. Draw a bridge table
    and 4 players
    as you were shown
    in BRIDGE ART.
37. Draw
    a BRIDGE
    HAND

38. What is the HIGH CARD POINT VALUE of these cards?
         A   K   Q   J
39. How many HCP are there in one suit?   in the deck?
40. How many HCP are there in each of the following hands:

a) ♠ KQ 10
   ♡ AJ 32
   ◇ 53
   ♣ 9764

d) ♠ J983
   ♡ 10 643
   ◇ Q97
   ♣ 52

b) ♠ 8
   ♡ KJ73
   ◇ KJ42
   ♣ KJ65

e) ♠ K96
   ♡ K93
   ◇ QJ42
   ♣ QJ10

c) ♠ AQJ
   ♡ AJ9632
   ◇ AK
   ♣ A5

f) ♠ Q9876
   ♡ 4
   ◇ Q1032
   ♣ J108

TEST YOURSELF

41. In bidding, what is meant by THE BOOK? _____
_____

42. If you bid the following, how many tricks
    are you promising to make?
    a) 1♣ ____   h) 1◇ ____
    b) 2◇ ____   i) 3♠ ____
    c) 3♡ ____   j) 7◇ ____
    d) 3NT ____   k) 2NT ____
    e) 4♡ ____   l) 5♣ ____
    f) 6NT ____   m) 4♠ ____
    g) 7♠ ____   n) 3♡ ____

43. Write out all the 1-level bids. _____
_____

44. Write out all the 6-level bids. _____
_____

45. How many bidding levels are there? _____
46. What do you say when you don't want to bid? _____
47. When is the bidding over? _____
48. What is the main rule about bidding? _____
49. In what direction does the bidding go? _____
50. Who starts the bidding? _____
51. How many bids are there altogether? _____
52. How many bids on each level? _____
53. What is the contract? _____
_____

54. What does the contract tell us? _____
_____

55. Which kind of contract scores the fewest points? _____
56. Why are GAME CONTRACTS special? _____
57. What is the GAME CONTRACT for:
    a) ♣ _____   c) ♡ _____   e) NT _____
    b) ◇ _____   d) ♠ _____

58. How many tricks do you need to win to make:
    a) a MINOR SUIT game? _____
    b) a MAJOR SUIT game? _____
    c) a NO TRUMP game? _____

TEST YOURSELF

59. Why are the MINOR SUITS unpopular as contracts?
_____

60. What is the RULE about GAME CONTRACTS?_____
_____

61. What are all the SMALL SLAM contracts?
_____

62. What are all the GRAND SLAM contracts?
_____

63. How many tricks do you need to make a SMALL SLAM?_____ a GRAND SLAM?_____

64. How many tricks can you lose and still make your SMALL SLAM?_____ your GRAND SLAM?____

65. Who gets the title of DECLARER?_____
_____

66. Who becomes DUMMY?_____
_____

67. Who makes the OPENING LEAD?_____
_____

68. When does DUMMY go down on the table?_____
_____

69. Who plays cards from the DUMMY?_____
_____

70. Who are the DEFENDERS?_____
_____

71. What are the DEFENDERS trying to do?_____
_____

72. What does GOING DOWN mean?_____
_____

73. What does MAKING YOUR CONTRACT mean?
_____

74. What are TWO REASONS for BIDDING?
_____
_____

75. What is a FIT?_____

76. Why do you need a fit in order to pick trump?____
_____

77. What are 4 different kinds of FITS?
_____

BIDDING IS A LANGUAGE

part two

the opening bid

The first bid made
in the bidding is called
the OPENING BID.
The DEALER gets the first chance to make
the opening bid, but if his hand isn't good enough,
he will pass. The next to bid (to the left, right?)
will have a turn, and so on. If NOBODY can make
an opening bid, the cards are thrown in, shuffled again
and re-dealt by the new dealer.
Whoever bids FIRST is the OPENING BIDDER.

the response

If you open
the bidding, then your partner
is called the RESPONDER.
The RESPONSE is always the answer
to the OPENING BID.
To respond means to ANSWER.
In a way, the RESPONDER is answering
The OPENING BID.
The RESPONDER is always the partner
of the OPENER.

the opening bid

✻ ✻ ✻ ✻ ✻ COUNT YOUR POINTS ✻ ✻ ✻ ✻ ✻

⭐ You must have **13** HCP or more before you can OPEN the bidding. ⭐

THERE ARE 3 KINDS OF OPENING HANDS

All opening hands have **13** or more High Card Points.

THE MINI OPENING HAND

THE MINI OPENING HAND HAS 13 OR 14 HIGH CARD POINTS.

THE MEDIUM OPENING HAND

THE MEDIUM OPENING HAND HAS 15, 16, OR 17 HIGH CARD POINTS.

THE MAXI OPENING HAND

THE MAXI OPENING HAND HAS 18 OR MORE HIGH CARD POINTS

WHAT DO YOU KNOW ?

Count up the HIGH CARD POINTS. Answer the questions. Is the hand an opening hand?
If so, what kind of opening hand is it?

1. ♠ KQ
   ♡ Q
   ◇ A 10 7 6 5
   ♣ KJ965

   How many HCP? _____
   Is it an opening hand? _____
   Which kind of opening hand? _____

2. ♠ Q872
   ♡ 652
   ◇ AK6
   ♣ J 10 5

   How many HCP? _____
   Is it an opening hand? _____
   Which kind of opening hand? _____

3. ♠ A76
   ♡ AK 10 3
   ◇ Q 3 2
   ♣ 943

   How many HCP? _____
   Is it an opening hand? _____
   Which kind of opening hand? _____

4. ♠ QJ 10 5
   ♡ AKJ
   ◇ AQ 10
   ♣ K 10 4

   How many HCP? _____
   Is it an opening hand? _____
   Which kind of opening hand? _____

5. ♠ 53
   ♡ Q954
   ◇ Q 10 9 7
   ♣ 842

   How many HCP? _____
   Is it an opening hand? _____
   Which kind of opening hand? _____

6. ♠ KQ842
   ♡ K7
   ◇ J5
   ♣ A854

   How many HCP? _____
   Is it an opening hand? _____
   Which kind of opening hand? _____

7. How many High Card Points do you need before you can open the hand? _____

THE MINI OPENER

So you have 13 or 14 high card points.
You know you can open the hand.
What bid do you make?
Just follow these simple steps!

⭐1 DO YOU HAVE A LONG MAJOR SUIT?

If you have a major suit with 5 or more cards,

BID 1♡ OR 1♠ But when you don't have a 5 or more card major suit —

⭐2 WHICH IS YOUR LONGER MINOR SUIT?
If you **DON'T** have a 5-card or longer MAJOR suit you can bid ONE of your longer MINOR:

BID 1♣ OR 1♢ But what if you have two minor suits? —

⭐3 ARE YOUR MINORS THE SAME LENGTH?
If you DON'T have a 5-card or longer MAJOR suit, AND your MINOR suits are the SAME LENGTH,

BID 1♣ WITH **3** CARDS IN EACH MINOR.

BID 1♢ WITH **4** OR MORE CARDS IN EACH MINOR.

Now, as we teach you how to bid, we are teaching you a way to bid called **5-CARD MAJORS.**

Bidding this way, you never open a MAJOR suit unless you have 5 or more cards in that major.

Remember when we explained that MINOR SUIT CONTRACTS were less popular? Because of this, you want to first look for a **MAJOR SUIT FIT** when you are bidding.
When you open 1♡ or 1♠, your PARTNER knows you have AT LEAST a 5-CARD SUIT. Partner knows to look for the 3 or more cards in that major to make a FIT.

What is your Opening Bid?

DRAW THE IN THE CIRCLE ANSWER

1. ♠ AK 10 9 4
   ♡ K 5 2
   ◇ Q 9
   ♣ Q 10 9

2. ♠ 10 7 4
   ♡ AQ10 6 3
   ◇ 10
   ♣ AK 8 4

3. ♠ Q 9 5
   ♡ J 8 3
   ◇ AQ 5 4
   ♣ A 9 8

4. ♠ QJ 10 2
   ♡ K 4 3
   ◇ AK 9 4 2
   ♣ 9

5. ♠ A 9 5
   ♡ AJ 8 6 5
   ◇ QJ 8 3
   ♣ J

6. ♠ KJ 10 3
   ♡ Q 10 5 2
   ◇ A 7 6
   ♣ A 3

7. ♠ KJ 10
   ♡ KQ 10 6
   ◇ A 7 2
   ♣ 9 8 2

8. ♠ AJ 10 5 4 3
   ♡ QJ 9
   ◇ A 10
   ♣ J 4

9. ♠ A
   ♡ QJ 9 8
   ◇ KJ 9 3
   ♣ Q 10 4 2

10. ♠ KJ 9 3
    ♡ KJ 10 5
    ◇ K
    ♣ Q 7 6 4

74

THE MEDIUM OPENER

BALANCED HANDS

A BALANCED HAND
is one which has
- NO 5-CARD OR LONGER MAJOR
- NO <u>SINGLETONS</u> OR <u>VOIDS</u>
- NO MORE THAN ONE DOUBLETON

a singleton is a suit which
has only ONE CARD.

a void is a suit
which has NO CARDS.

a doubleton is a suit
which has only TWO CARDS.

If you have a
MEDIUM opener
and a BALANCED
HAND you can
OPEN

1NT
ONE NO TRUMP

Making an opening bid of **1NT** says to partner
"HEY – I HAVE 15-17 POINTS, AND
A BALANCED HAND.
OF COURSE, I HAVE NO 5-CARD MAJOR."

If you have a MEDIUM OPENER, but not a BALANCED
HAND, you open the bidding in the same way as you
did with a MINI OPENER.

1. Open 1♡ or 1♤ if you have 5 or more.
2. Open your LONGER MINOR - 1♧ or 1♢.
3. Open 1♢ with four or more cards in each minor suit.
4. Open 1♧ with 3 cards in each minor suit.

What is your Opening Bid?

1. ♠ KQ3
   ♡ A3
   ◇ KQJ94
   ♣ J86
   (1NT)

2. ♠ AJ872
   ♡ QJ8
   ◇ A765
   ♣ Q

3. ♠ K3
   ♡ AQ1064
   ◇ A75
   ♣ A52

4. ♠ A103
   ♡ AQJ
   ◇ KJ42
   ♣ Q109

5. ♠ Q98
   ♡ KQ106
   ◇ Q2
   ♣ J1082

6. ♠ A863
   ♡ 1076
   ◇ A98
   ♣ AQ10

7. ♠ AK7
   ♡ 1042
   ◇ AQ
   ♣ KJ1076

8. ♠ Q985
   ♡ K7
   ◇ KJ96
   ♣ A84

9. ♠ A98
   ♡ KQ1063
   ◇ Q2
   ♣ Q108

10. ♠ AK1043
    ♡ 94
    ◇ A64
    ♣ A73

11. ♠ 764
    ♡ KJ1063
    ◇ K103
    ♣ Q5

12. ♠ AQ2
    ♡ K965
    ◇ KQ9
    ♣ 1087

13. ♠ K10862
    ♡ QJ92
    ◇ A5
    ♣ AK

14. ♠ K42
    ♡ AKQ1094
    ◇ K32
    ♣ 4

15. ♠ AQ73
    ♡ AQ9
    ◇ Q53
    ♣ Q106

16. ♠ 105
    ♡ 63
    ◇ A65
    ♣ AKQJ86

THE MAXI OPENER 18 OR MORE HCP

BALANCED HANDS

Remember — no singletons or voids, no more than one doubleton.
— no 5-card or longer major

IF YOU HAVE A BALANCED HAND, YOU BID LIKE THIS:

18-20 HCP	Open 1♣ or 1◇, then later JUMP a level of bidding in NT to show a BIG hand. More on this later.
21-24 HCP	Open **2 NT**
25-28 HCP	Open **3 NT**
29-31 HCP	Open **4 NT**
32-33 HCP	Open **5 NT**
34-36 HCP	Open **6 NT**
37 HCP	Open **7 NT** (You can't hold more than 37)

UNBALANCED HANDS

IF YOU HAVE 18-20 HCP OPEN ONE OF A SUIT LIKE YOU WOULD HAVE WITH A MINI OPENER, AND LATER JUMP A LEVEL OF BIDDING WHEN IT'S YOUR NEXT TURN TO BID.

IF YOU HAVE 21 OR MORE HCP AND YOU HAVE AN UNBALANCED HAND, YOU BID LIKE THIS:

2♡ or 2♠ WITH A 5-CARD OR LONGER SUIT.

2♣ or 2◇ WITH A 5-CARD OR LONGER SUIT.

THESE ARE CALLED **STRONG TWO BIDS!**

What is your Opening Bid?

1. ♠ AKQ1042
   ♡ A
   ◇ KQ3
   ♣ QJ10

2. ♠ AQ
   ♡ KJ104
   ◇ KQJ
   ♣ AJ109

3. ♠ AKQJ
   ♡ AKJ
   ◇ AKQ10
   ♣ AK

4. ♠ AK10
   ♡ AQJ1094
   ◇ KJ10
   ♣ 3

5. ♠ AQ109
   ♡ KQJ5
   ◇ K10
   ♣ KQ7

6. ♠ AQJ10
   ♡ KQJ4
   ◇ K10
   ♣ KQ7

7. ♠ AJ10
   ♡ KQ9
   ◇ AKJ75
   ♣ KQ

8. ♠ 54
   ♡ AKQ1042
   ◇ AQ
   ♣ AK10

9. ♠ AK
   ♡ AKQJ
   ◇ AQ109
   ♣ AQ10

10. ♠ VOID
    ♡ AK9
    ◇ AQJ1093
    ♣ KQ42

11. ♠ AK9
    ♡ KQ43
    ◇ 3
    ♣ AKJ109

12. ♠ A
    ♡ AK8
    ◇ 3
    ♣ AQJ98542

FUN WITH WORDS

Bridge players have their very own special words and phrases when they are telling stories about the game.

For example, instead of saying you had "5 spades with the A and K", you would say, "I had AK fifth." See if you can match the phrase on the left with the suits on the right.

AK FIFTH	1095432	6♠ WITH THE TEN AND NINE
QJ THIRD	KQ	THE KING AND QUEEN ALONE
STIFF K	QJ4	3♠ WITH THE QUEEN AND JACK
RAG DUB	10	A SINGLETON TEN
KQ TIGHT	32	A DOUBLETON WITH NO HONORS
STIFF 10	Q8	A DOUBLETON WITH THE QUEEN
Q DUB	K	A SINGLETON KING
109 SIXTH	AK763	5♠ WITH THE ACE AND KING

THERE ARE MANY OTHER PHRASES BRIDGE PLAYERS USE. THESE PHRASES CHANGE FROM PLACE TO PLACE BUT ALL DESCRIBE BRIDGE HANDS AND BIDDING.

The contract was COLD.
The contract was ICY.

The contract would never go down.

He went into the TANK.
He went into the CLOSET.

He sat and thought for a while.

Dummy FLOPPED.

The dummy was put on the table.

It's fun to talk this way. Try it!
Describe this hand. You don't have to say the suits, just give your ♠s first, then your ♡s, then ◇s, then ♣s.

♠ QJ103 _____
♡ K _____
◇ AK _____
♣ AQJ1094 _____

the response

THE **RESPONSE** HAPPENS
AFTER PARTNER HAS MADE AN **OPENING BID**.
NOW, IF YOU CAN, YOU MUST MAKE A
RESPONDING BID, TO HELP YOUR TEAM.

THINK HARD. YOU KNOW A LOT ABOUT OPENER'S
HAND. THERE'S AT LEAST 13 POINTS ACROSS
FROM YOU, AND A SUIT. IF THE OPENER'S BID
WAS **NT**, THERE ARE EVEN MORE POINTS
AND A BALANCED HAND OVER THERE.

LOOK at your hand.

HOW MANY POINTS DO YOU HAVE?
ADD TO THEM THE NUMBER OF POINTS
YOUR PARTNER HAS PROMISED.

IF THE TOTAL OF THESE POINTS IS
MORE THAN 25 OF THE HCP
IN THE WHOLE DECK, YOU AND PARTNER
MIGHT BE ABLE TO WIN ENOUGH TRICKS
TO MAKE A **GAME CONTRACT**
AND GET YOUR **BONUS SCORE**.

26 HCP = 3NT 4♡ 4♠

IF YOU AND YOUR PARTNER HAVE 26 OR SO HCP
YOU SHOULD BE ABLE TO **BID** AND **MAKE**
GAME IN 3NT, 4♡, OR 4♠.

28 HCP = 5♣ 5♢

IF YOU AND YOUR PARTNER HAVE
28 OR SO YOU SHOULD BE ABLE TO **BID**
AND MAKE **GAME** IN A **MINOR SUIT**.

5♣ OR 5♢

THERE ARE 40 HCP IN THE WHOLE DECK.

 If you and your partner have 26 or more HCP, you can probably make a game.

 If you and your partner have 30 or more HCP, you can probably make a slam.

THINK OF THE DECK AS A PIE!

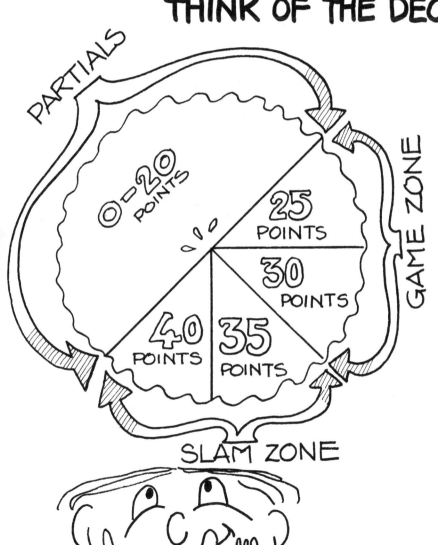

PARTIALS

GAME ZONE

0-20 POINTS

25 POINTS

30 POINTS

40 POINTS

35 POINTS

SLAM ZONE

YUM

When Partner opens the bidding, you know right away about how many points he has. Now — You have two duties to help your team win the bidding.

 Tell opener if you have a FIT.

 Tell opener about YOUR hand.

the response

COUNT YOUR POINTS

☆ ⑥ HCP OR MORE TO MAKE A RESPONDING BID.

THERE ARE 3 KINDS OF RESPONDING HANDS

THE MINI RESPONDING HAND

6 TO 9 POINTS

THE MINI RESPONDING HAND HAS 6, 7, 8, OR 9 HCP.

THE MEDIUM RESPONDING HAND

10 TO 12 POINTS

THE MEDIUM RESPONDING HAND HAS 10, 11, OR 12 HCP.

THE MAXI RESPONDING HAND

13 OR MORE POINTS

THE MAXI RESPONDING HAND HAS 13 HCP OR MORE.

THE FIT

We have talked a lot about FITS

As RESPONDER, you must let OPENER know if you have a FIT for the suit OPENER has BID. If 1♡ or 1♤ was opened, in bidding language, that means:

☆ 13 OR MORE POINTS

☆ 5 OR MORE ♡'s OR ♤'s

So, if you have 3 or more cards in OPENER'S MAJOR you want to show the FIT. Also, it would be nice to show how many points you have. This is EASY to do!

THE MINI RESPONDING HAND

(6 TO 9 HCP) Raise opener's suit ONE LEVEL
Bid 2♡ or 2♤ after partner has bid 1♡ or 1♤.

THE MEDIUM RESPONDING HAND

(10 TO 12 HCP) Raise opener's suit TWO LEVELS.
Bid 3♡ or 3♤ after partner has bid 1♡ or 1♤.

THESE BIDS TELL OPENER **2** THINGS.

⟹ YOU HAVE A FIT FOR ♡'s OR ♤'s

⟹ YOU HAVE 6-9 HCP IF YOU BID 2♡ OR 2♤
OR,
YOU HAVE 10-12 HCP IF YOU BID 3♡ OR 3♤

Now OPENER can look at his hand and decide if you should be in GAME, or try to be in GAME.

LIMIT BIDS

LIMIT BIDS
are bids which show
EXACTLY how many points
you have.
LIMIT BIDS say,
"Partner, I have no LESS
than _____ points and
I have no MORE than _____
points."
LIMIT BIDS
are good to use
when you can
because they help partner decide
what kind of contract
you should play.
If partner opens 1♠
and you respond 2♠
you have made a LIMIT BID
because your bid says,
"I have no less than 6 high card points
and no more than 9 high card points."
Of course, the same is true of 1♡-2♡.
If partner opens 1♠
and you respond 3♠ (or the bidding goes 1♡-3♡),
you have made a LIMIT BID
because your bid says,
"I have no less than 10 high card points
and no more than 12 high card points."

WATCH
FOR
LIMIT
BIDS!

➡ **LIMIT BIDS**
TELL PARTNER
EXACTLY HOW MANY POINTS
YOU COULD HAVE AND
HOW FEW POINTS YOU COULD HAVE.

Fun Page
SMARTY CAT

Whenever you learn something new, you learn a whole bunch of special words. Let's see if you can be a SMARTY CAT and connect each of the bridge words below with its meaning. Draw a line between them.

THE MINORS	THE TOP TO BOTTOM ORDER OF THE CARDS AND SUITS
THE BOOK	THE FIRST CARD PLAYED TO ANY TRICK
LIMIT BID	ONLY ONE CARD IN A SUIT
CONTRACT	DIAMONDS AND CLUBS
THE MAJORS	WHAT YOU SAY IF YOU DON'T WANT TO BID
GOING DOWN	THE FIRST PERSON TO MAKE A BID
GAMES	HIGH CARD POINTS USED TO COUNT BRIDGE HANDS
SINGLETON	NO CARDS AT ALL IN A SUIT
RANK	SPADES AND HEARTS
LEAD	A BID THAT PROMISES NO MORE THAN A CERTAIN NUMBER OF POINTS AND NO LESS THAN A CERTAIN NUMBER OF POINTS
TRUMP	MAKING LESS THAN THE NUMBER OF TRICKS PROMISED IN YOUR CONTRACT.
VOID	3NT, 4♡, 4♤, 5♧, 5♢
BALANCED HAND	TWO CARDS IN A SUIT
PASS	THE FINAL BID - PICKING TRUMP AND PROMISING TO TAKE A CERTAIN NUMBER OF TRICKS
RESPONDER	A HAND WITH NO SINGLETONS OR VOIDS AND NO MORE THAN ONE DOUBLETON
OPENER	A SUIT WHICH WINS A TRICK OVER ALL OTHER SUITS
HCP	THE OPENER'S PARTNER
ROUNDS	THE FIRST SIX TRICKS
DOUBLETON	FOUR BIDS WHERE EACH PLAYER GETS ONE TURN

85

When partner opens, the OPENING BID promises AT LEAST 13 HCP.
If you are RESPONDER and you have 13 HCP OR MORE

THEN YOU KNOW YOUR TEAM HAS 26 HCP OR MORE!

If partner OPENS and you have a hand that you could have OPENED if you had a chance, then make sure that your team gets to game.

13 + 13 = 26 ⟶ enough HCP for game

☆☆ **RULE** OPENER OPPOSITE OPENER SHOULD BE IN GAME.

Let's say your partner OPENED and you also have an OPENING hand. **IF OPENER OPENED 1♡ OR 1♠ AND YOU HAVE 3 OR MORE ♡ OR ♠, YOU HAVE A FIT.**

THE MAXI RESPONDING HAND

13 OR MORE HCP

IF YOU HAVE A **FIT** FOR OPENER'S MAJOR:

RAISE TO GAME!

BID **4♡ or 4♠** YOU HAVE A **FIT**, AND YOU HAVE AN **OPENING** HAND— AND PARTNER HAS AN **OPENING** HAND, YOU SHOULD BE IN GAME.

Review

If partner OPENS 1♡ or 1♠ and you have a **FIT**, RESPOND

► 2♡ (or 2♠) with a MINI RESPONDING HAND
  · 3 or more ♡ (or ♠)
  · 6 - 9 HCP
  ➧ THIS IS A **LIMIT BID**.

► 3♡ (or 3♠) with a MEDIUM RESPONDING HAND
  · 3 or more ♡ (or ♠)
  · 10 - 12 HCP
  ➧ THIS IS A **LIMIT BID**.

4♡ (or 4♠) with a MAXI RESPONDING HAND
  · 3 or more ♡ (or ♠)
  · 13 or more HCP

RAISE PARTNER'S SUIT TO ANOTHER LEVEL TO SHOW A FIT

TEST YOURSELF

1. Partner opens 1♡   your hand is
♠ J94
♡ QJ3
◇ A1094
♣ J83
you respond? _____

2. Partner opens 1♠   your hand is
♠ KJ43
♡ AK
◇ Q109
♣ J875
you respond? _____

3. Partner opens 1♠   your hand is
♠ KJ43
♡ A2
◇ Q10
♣ J1075
you respond? _____

THERE'S MORE TO DO ON THE NEXT PAGE

4. Partner opens 1♡ your hand is ♠ A3 ♡ KQ102 ◊ J1032 ♣ Q53 you respond? _____

5. Partner opens 1♡ your hand is ♠ A3 ♡ KQ102 ◊ KJ103 ♣ Q105 you respond? _____

6. Partner opens 1♠ your hand is ♠ A103 ♡ J98 ◊ K1084 ♣ 932 you respond? _____

7. What do you call the first bid made? _____

8. Who has the first chance to make an opening bid? _____

9. Who is the opening bidder? _____

10. If you open the bidding, then your partner is called the _____

11. How many HCP should you have before you open the bidding? _____

12. What are the 3 kinds of opening hands?
   a.)_____   ____to ____ HCP.
   b.)_____   ____to ____ HCP.
   c.)_____   ____to ____ HCP.

13. What is a BALANCED HAND? _____
_____

14. What is a SINGLETON? _____

15. What is a VOID? _____

16. What do you need in your hand to open 1NT? _____
_____

17. What do you need to open 2NT? _____

18. How many HCP do you need between you and your partner to be able to BID and MAKE GAME
   a) in 3NT, 4♡, or 4♠? _____
   b) in 5♣ or 5◊? _____

BUT What if I **DON'T** HAVE A FIT?

OPENER HAS OPENED 1♡ OR 1♠ AND YOU HAVE NO FIT...

THE MINI RESPONDING HAND

6 TO 9 POINTS

Take a look at your hand.
Let's say you have no fit for the MAJOR suit partner just opened. But you do have lots of other cards, right?
You want to tell partner about these cards, even though you can't help partner's suit.

☆☆ **RULE** YOU CAN **NOT** RESPOND A NEW SUIT ON THE 2-LEVEL UNLESS YOU HAVE 10 OR MORE POINTS.

☆ With a WEAK RESPONDING HAND, the ONLY time you can bid on the 2-level is when you have a **FIT**.

YOU BID 1NT IF YOU DO **NOT** HAVE A FIT.

1NT by RESPONDER is a LIMIT BID.

IT SHOWS 6-9 HCP AND NO FIT!

RESPONDING 1NT IS NOT LIKE OPENING 1NT.

IF OPENER BIDS 1♡
As RESPONDER you have 2 things you can bid.

1♤ if you have 4 or more ♤s.　　①

Even though you don't have a **FIT** for your partner's ♡s, partner just might have a **FIT** for YOUR ♤s.

You don't need 5♤s to respond 1♤ after partner opens 1♡. You only need 4♤s. You might have more, BUT you only need 4.

Opener will now look at his hand and see if he has a **FIT** with your ♤s.

Partner needs to have 4 cards in ♤s before there is a **FIT**.

4 + 4 = 8 and remember, that is a **FIT**!

Even though you don't have a fit for your partner's ♡s you should bid your ♤s if you have them.

You are still looking for a **FIT** somewhere.

That is the first thing you should check your hand for. The second thing is:

If you don't have 4 or more ♤s, you bid ——

1NT LIMIT BID　　②

This says:
- ◆ You have 6-9 HCP
- ◆ You have no **FIT**
- ◆ You have fewer than 4♤s.

Review　MINI RESPONDING HANDS　（6-9 HCP）

Opener opens 1♡
- ✳ Bid 2♡ with a **FIT** (LIMIT BID).
- ✳ Bid 1♤ with 4 or more.
- ✳ Bid 1NT with less than 4♤ and no **FIT** (LIMIT).

Opener opens 1♤
- ✳ Bid 2♤ with a **FIT** (LIMIT BID).
- ✳ Bid 1NT with no **FIT** (LIMIT BID).

♣ REMEMBER ♣

PARTNER OPENS 1♡

Bid 2♡ with a fit.
Bid 1♠ with 4 or more.
Bid 1NT with less than
   4♠s and no fit

PARTNER OPENS 1♠

Bid 2♠ with a fit.

Bid 1NT with no fit.

☾ ☆ WHAT DO YOU KNOW ? ☆ ☽

1. PARTNER OPENS 1♠

♠ KJ103
♡ A2
◇ J942
♣ 1064

I respond: _____
My response says: _____
_____
_____

2. PARTNER OPENS 1♡

♠ KJ10
♡ A2
◇ J942
♣ 10964

I respond: _____
My response says: _____
_____
_____

3. PARTNER OPENS 1♠

♠ Q105
♡ 92
◇ K942
♣ Q1096

I respond: _____
My response says: _____
_____
_____

4. PARTNER OPENS 1♡

♠ 5432
♡ A3
◇ K942
♣ 1096

I respond: _____
My response says: _____
_____
_____

5. PARTNER OPENS 1♡

♠ 52
♡ KJ
◇ J1032
♣ A10984

I respond: _____
My response says: _____
_____
_____

6. How many HCP are needed to respond at the 2-level? _____
7. Why do you want to respond 1♠ if you have 4♠s? _____
_____

THE MEDIUM RESPONDING HAND

10 11 OR 12 POINTS

IF OPENER OPENS 1♡ or 1♠

➡ BID 3♡ OR 3♠ TO SHOW A **FIT** AND 10-12 HCP.

YOU KNOW THIS ALREADY.

➡ Bid a NEW SUIT, if you have no fit for partner's MAJOR, you may find a fit somewhere else!

EXPLORE!

YOU WANT TO EXPLORE AND HUNT FOR A FIT.

Bid your longest suit. If you have two long suits bid the HIGHER RANKING SUIT FIRST.

If you have only 4-card suits bid them UP THE LADDER.

Bid whichever suit comes FIRST on the BIDDING LADDER.

1♠ comes before 2♣.

2♣ comes before 2♢, 2♢ comes before 2♡, and so on. If OPENER has a fit now, he will show it by RAISING your suit to another level depending on what kind of hand he has. If OPENER has no fit, he will **EXPLORE**.

REMEMBER YOU NEED 10 HCP OR MORE TO BID ON THE 2-LEVEL, SO WHEN YOU DO, YOU TELL PARTNER IMPORTANT THINGS ABOUT YOUR HAND.

think

IF YOU HAVE A **MEDIUM RESPONDING HAND** WHY CAN YOU **NEVER** RESPOND 1 NO TRUMP ?

YOU'RE RIGHT! BECAUSE THAT WOULD SAY YOU ONLY HAVE 6-9 HCP, AND YOU HAVE **MORE**.

THE MAXI RESPONDING HANDS

13 OR MORE HCP

If you have a **LONG SUIT** you can bid it **DON'T WORRY** about partner passing **BECAUSE**

OPENER PROMISES
TO BID AGAIN.

Whenever you or partner opens the bidding you are promising to bid at least one more time before you pass.

The **ONLY TIME** opener **DOESN'T** have to bid again is when RESPONDER has made a **LIMIT BID**

If you are RESPONDER, you can bid your long suit or 4-card suits at the one level EVEN if you have LOTS and LOTS of points! Partner will NEVER pass. NOW, if you are lucky, partner might even show you

A FIT.

THE MAXI RESPONDING HANDS

(13 OR MORE HCP)

THESE HANDS HAVE AS MANY POINTS AS AN OPENING HAND, OR MORE. MAYBE EVEN MANY MORE.

➤ (with a FIT for PARTNER'S MAJOR, bid GAME.)

WITH NO FIT FOR PARTNER'S MAJOR —

➤ (BID A NEW SUIT with 4 or more cards in the suit.)

If you have a LONG SUIT, you will want to bid it.

BUT, if you only have 4-card suits bid them
UP-THE-LADDER.

➤ (You want to **EXPLORE** and find your **FIT**.)

☆☆ RULE   ANYTIME RESPONDER BIDS A NEW SUIT
OPENER CAN **NOT** PASS AT HIS NEXT TURN TO BID. THIS IS SO YOU DON'T HAVE TO WORRY THAT YOU WON'T GET TO GAME. NEW SUITS ARE NOT **LIMIT BIDS**, RIGHT ?

➤ (YOU COULD BID **2NT** WITH A BALANCED HAND.)

If you bid 2NT you are showing a MAXI responding hand. Partner must now bid until GAME is reached. A response of 2NT is FORCING TO GAME!

Responding 2NT tells partner a lot of things about your hand.
   It says you do NOT HAVE A FIT for partner's MAJOR.
   It says you do NOT HAVE a 5-card or longer suit.
   It says you do NOT HAVE a 4-card MAJOR suit.
      If you did have a 4-card major, you would have EXPLORED by bidding 4-card suits UP-THE-LADDER.

What is your Response?

DRAW THE IN THE ANSWER CIRCLE

Partner opens 1♡

1. ♠ 43
   ♡ J4
   ◇ AQJ42
   ♣ AQ32

2. ♠ AK9865
   ♡ 986
   ◇ K32
   ♣ 9

3. ♠ KJ63
   ♡ 109
   ◇ K95
   ♣ KJ94

4. ♠ K109
   ♡ AJ8
   ◇ 862
   ♣ KQJ10

5. ♠ 5432
   ♡ AK
   ◇ QJ109
   ♣ Q103

6. ♠ K32
   ♡ A9
   ◇ QJ109
   ♣ 9863

7. ♠ 1093
   ♡ A3
   ◇ AQ109632
   ♣ 10

8. ♠ A103
   ♡ A3
   ◇ K1094
   ♣ J982

Partner opens 1♠

1. ♠ A10
   ♡ KJ43
   ◇ Q1092
   ♣ J103

2. ♠ 92
   ♡ K10932
   ◇ AK63
   ♣ J10

3. ♠ K2
   ♡ K109
   ◇ A10632
   ♣ J103

4. ♠ 92
   ♡ AK1093
   ◇ A1063
   ♣ K10

5. ♠ Q
   ♡ A532
   ◇ K1093
   ♣ 10985

6. ♠ A
   ♡ KJ43
   ◇ Q1092
   ♣ J1093

95

all the responding bids

WHEN PARTNER OPENS 1♡

MINI
RESPONDING HAND
6 TO 9 HCP

- 2♡ WITH A FIT **LIMIT BID**
- 1♠ WITH 4 OR MORE ♠s, NO **FIT**
- 1NT WITH NO FIT, NO 4 ♠s. **LIMIT**

MEDIUM
RESPONDING HAND
10 TO 12 HCP

- 3♡ WITH A FIT **LIMIT**
- 1♠, 2♣, or 2♢–BID YOUR LONG SUIT.
  OR BID 4-CARD SUITS UP-THE-LADDER.

MAXI
RESPONDING HAND
13+ HCP

- 4♡ WITH A FIT
- BID A LONG SUIT
  OR BID 4-CARD SUITS UP-THE-LADDER
- 2NT WITH NO FIT, NO 4-CARD MAJOR
  AND A BALANCED HAND.

WHEN PARTNER OPENS 1♠

MINI
6 TO 9

- 2♠ WITH A FIT **LIMIT**
- 1NT WITH NO FIT **LIMIT**

MEDIUM
10 TO 12

- 3♠ WITH A FIT
- 2♣, 2♢, 2♡ – BID YOUR LONG SUIT,
  OR BID 4-CARD SUITS UP-THE-LADDER.

MAXI
13+

- 4♠ WITH A FIT
- BID A LONG SUIT,
  OR BID 4-CARD SUITS UP-THE-LADDER.
- 2NT WITH NO FIT, NO 4-CARD MAJOR
  AND A BALANCED HAND.

What is your Response?

ALL RESPONSES
TO 1♡ OR 1♠

think

1. Tell opener if you have a fit.
2. Tell opener about your hand.

PARTNER OPENS 1♡

1. ♠ QJ6
   ♡ K873
   ◇ K85
   ♣ A63

2. ♠ 5432
   ♡ A6
   ◇ QJ106
   ♣ K72

3. ♠ A86
   ♡ 54
   ◇ 432
   ♣ AQ1063

4. ♠ J984
   ♡ J72
   ◇ 7
   ♣ 109763

5. ♠ K76
   ♡ A5
   ◇ KJ42
   ♣ A852

6. ♠ AK6
   ♡ A5
   ◇ KQJ32
   ♣ 982

7. ♠ A106
   ♡ KJ32
   ◇ 32
   ♣ J1097

8. ♠ AKJ52
   ♡ A3
   ◇ Q109
   ♣ J109

9. ♠ A32
   ♡ 109
   ◇ K1043
   ♣ A1097

10. ♠ 1098
    ♡ 9
    ◇ AKJ93
    ♣ 10982

11. ♠ J982
    ♡ Q106
    ◇ KJ94
    ♣ 108

12. ♠ A93
    ♡ KQ10
    ◇ J109
    ♣ Q1093

What is your Response?

ALL RESPONSES TO 1♡ OR 1♤

PARTNER OPENS 1♤

1. ♤ A6
   ♡ 743
   ◇ QJ10974
   ♧ AQ

2. ♤ K1095
   ♡ AJ8
   ◇ 562
   ♧ KJ7

3. ♤ QJ
   ♡ A10984
   ◇ J1098
   ♧ A2

4. ♡ QJ
   ♡ A1098
   ◇ J1098
   ♧ A93

5. ♤ 1098
   ♡ AJ3
   ◇ J109
   ♧ Q832

6. ♤ 109
   ♡ AJ103
   ◇ J109
   ♧ Q832

7. ♤ A62
   ♡ QJ105
   ◇ K10
   ♧ Q632

8. ♤ A62
   ♡ QJ10
   ◇ K10932
   ♧ Q3

9. ♤ 432
   ♡ J103
   ◇ 1098
   ♧ AKQJ

10. ♤ 43
    ♡ J1032
    ◇ 1098
    ♧ AKQJ

11. ♤ 43
    ♡ J103
    ◇ 1098
    ♧ AKQJ2

12. ♤ A3
    ♡ J103
    ◇ 1098
    ♧ AKJ105

13. ♤ K3
    ♡ A1098
    ◇ J109
    ♧ A932

14. ♤ 432
    ♡ AK109
    ◇ QJ10
    ♧ AK3

PARTNER OPENS 1♣ OR 1♦

When partner opens a MINOR SUIT
THINK about what you know:

- ◆ partner has 13 or more points.
- ◆ partner has no 5-card major.

AND ◆ He may have ONLY 3 CARDS IN THE MINOR SUIT HE OPENED

WHY? ◆ There are hands that have to be opened 1♣ or 1♦ even with only 3 cards in the MINOR.

♠ xxxx		Pretend this hand has 13 points. Opener can't open a MAJOR so he opens his <u>longer</u> MINOR, which is 1♦ – a 3-card suit.
♡ xxxx		
♢ xxx		
♣ xx		

♠ xxxx		The same with this hand. Opener bids 1♣ because there are 3 cards in each MINOR suit.
♡ xxx		
♢ xxx		
♣ xxx		

♧ REMEMBER ♧

When the OPENER bids 1♣ or 1♦ there may be as few as 3 cards in the suit!

SO YOU MUST HAVE AT LEAST 5 CARDS IN ♣s or ♦s BEFORE YOU CAN BE SURE OF A FIT (5+3=8)

responding hands

MINI RESPONDING HAND

(6-9 HCP)

➡ **BID YOUR LONG SUIT**

But don't bid on the 2-level.
Why? - Right! Because you don't have
10 or more High Card Points.

➡ **BID 4-CARD SUITS** UP-THE LADDER.

If you don't have a long suit, you can
respond by bidding a 4-card suit
up-the-ladder. Bid the lowest-ranking
4-card suit first. Remember the
BIDDING LADDER? ♣s, then ♦s, then ♥s, then ♠s.

➡ **BID 1NT - A LIMIT BID**

If you have no long suit and no 4-CARD
MAJOR, bid 1NT. This is a LIMIT BID which says
no less than 6 HCP and no more than 9 HCP.

➡ **SHOW A FIT** FOR PARTNER'S MINOR

RAISE PARTNER'S MINOR TO THE 2-LEVEL.
LIMIT. THIS SHOWS 6 to 9 HCP and
5 CARDS OR MORE in opener's MINOR.

IT'S A
GOOD IDEA Bid 1♥ or 1♠ before
you show a FIT for
opener's minor. YOU WANT
to find a MAJOR SUIT FIT.

What is your Response?

Responses to 1♣/1◇ with MINI Responding Hands.
- ◆ Bid your long suit.
- ◆ Bid 4-card suits up-the-ladder.
- ◆ Bid 1NT LIMIT.
- ◆ Show a fit.

PARTNER OPENS 1♣

1. ♠ A1042
   ♡ J32
   ◇ KJ93
   ♣ 10 9

2. ♠ A1042
   ♡ J532
   ◇ KJ93
   ♣ 10

3. ♠ A1042
   ♡ J532
   ◇ KJ9
   ♣ 103

4. ♠ A104
   ♡ J105
   ◇ KJ9
   ♣ 10 532

5. ♠ A104
   ♡ J10
   ◇ KJ9
   ♣ 109 532

6. ♠ A1042
   ♡ KJ 1032
   ◇ J10
   ♣ 109

7. ♠ K103
   ♡ KJ1032
   ◇ Q1063
   ♣ 9

8. ♠ K10532
   ♡ KJ103
   ◇ Q10
   ♣ 92

9. ♠ AKJ10
   ♡ 9863
   ◇ J103
   ♣ 92

10. ♠ A103
    ♡ QJ9
    ◇ 1093
    ♣ Q1032

11. ♠ A3
    ♡ QJ93
    ◇ 109
    ♣ Q10432

12. ♠ A10
    ♡ QJ10
    ◇ 1093
    ♣ Q10432

responding hands

MEDIUM RESPONDING HAND

10-12 HCP

→ **BID YOUR LONG SUIT**

You can bid on the 2-level if you want because you have more than 10 HCP.

→ **SHOW A FIT** RAISE PARTNER'S MINOR

Show your FIT for PARTNER'S MINOR by raising the suit to the 3-level if you have 5+ of his minor. This is a **LIMIT BID** promising 10-12 HCP **BUT** it also shows no **4-CARD MAJOR**.

★ **RULE** ABOUT **LIMIT BIDS**

When partner opens a minor suit 1♣ or 1♦, ALWAYS bid a MAJOR SUIT (if you have one) BEFORE YOU MAKE A LIMIT BID.

→ When partner opens a minor suit your first job is to

EXPLORE! and try to find a major suit fit.

What is your Response?

Responding to 1♣/1◇ with MEDIUM RESPONDING HANDS. Bid your long suit. Bid 4-card suits up-the-ladder. Show a FIT by raising to the 3-level.

PARTNER OPENS 1♣

1. ♠ 32
   ♡ K983
   ◇ AQ10
   ♣ K742

2. ♠ 62
   ♡ AK1076
   ◇ QJ98
   ♣ J2

3. ♠ AK109
   ♡ QJ87
   ◇ 5432
   ♣ Q

4. ♠ AK10
   ♡ QJ8
   ◇ 5432
   ♣ Q109

5. ♠ AK10
   ♡ QJ8
   ◇ 43
   ♣ Q10932

6. ♠ KJ1094
   ♡ Q1093
   ◇ A4
   ♣ 109

PARTNER OPENS 1◇

1. ♠ KQJ10
   ♡ 10832
   ◇ J104
   ♣ K3

2. ♠ 62
   ♡ Q92
   ◇ AQJ9
   ♣ QJ102

3. ♠ K73
   ♡ A105
   ◇ Q85
   ♣ J943

4. ♠ K732
   ♡ A1054
   ◇ Q8
   ♣ QJ9

5. ♠ K7632
   ♡ A1054
   ◇ Q8
   ♣ QJ

6. ♠ K732
   ♡ A10
   ◇ K10932
   ♣ J9

responding hands

STRONG RESPONDING HAND

(13 HCP OR MORE)

BID A LONG SUIT

REMEMBER, OPENER cannot PASS.

BID 4-CARD SUITS UP-THE-LADDER

Just like all other kinds of responding hands, you want to find a MAJOR SUIT FIT.

remember

OPENER WILL NEVER PASS IF YOU BID A NEW SUIT. YOU WILL ALWAYS GET ANOTHER CHANCE TO BID!

BID 2 NT - FORCING

This shows 13 or more points and NO 4-CARD OR LONGER MAJOR. This also shows a balanced hand. This bid is FORCING TO GAME.

SHOW A FIT FOR PARTNER'S MINOR

If you have 5 or more cards in partner's minor suit AND you have no MAJOR suit 4-cards long (or longer):

Bid the other minor and then jump in partner's suit at your next turn to bid.

What is your Response?

Responding to 1♣/1◇ with a MAXI RESPONDING HAND.
Bid a long suit.
Bid 4-card suits up-the-ladder
Bid 2NT(no 4-card major.)
Bid the other minor suit, planning to bid partner's minor suit at the 3-level on the next round to show a FIT.

PARTNER OPENS 1♣

1. ♠ AK9
   ♡ QJ32
   ◇ K53
   ♣ 1063

2. ♠ AK853
   ♡ Q4
   ◇ 1092
   ♣ AJ6

3. ♠ 32
   ♡ KJ83
   ◇ AQ10
   ♣ K742

4. ♠ Q54
   ♡ A4
   ◇ A874
   ♣ A953

5. ♠ KJ10
   ♡ 8
   ◇ KQ3
   ♣ AJ10986

6. ♠ A103
   ♡ KQ93
   ◇ AJ102
   ♣ 109

PARTNER OPENS 1◇

1. ♠ AQJ83
   ♡ VOID
   ◇ KQ5
   ♣ KJ1074

2. ♠ A103
   ♡ J10
   ◇ KQ5
   ♣ KJ1074

3. ♠ A103
   ♡ J102
   ◇ KQ5
   ♣ KJ107

4. ♠ A103
   ♡ KQ93
   ◇ AJ102
   ♣ 109

5. ♠ Q54
   ♡ A4
   ◇ A874
   ♣ A953

6. ♠ QJ109
   ♡ KQ87
   ◇ A9
   ♣ K109

How many HCP do partner and I need to make game in 3NT, 5♣, or 5◇?

think page

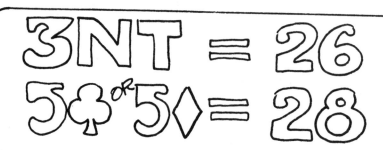

3NT = 26
5♣ or 5◇ = 28

Minor suit games need more points because you need to win more tricks than any other game.

If partner opens 1♣ or 1◇ you know that means at least 13 high card points.

If you have 13 or 14 points, your hands may not add up to enough for game in 5♣ or 5◇, so you want to EXPLORE to see if you can make 3NT.

Now, if partner opens, and you have 13 HCP, you know you have at least 26 HCP.

 IT'S A

GOOD IDEA

When you have a MAXI HAND and a fit for opener's minor suit LOOK at your hand.

Is it BALANCED? If it is, maybe you should bid 2NT. If it is UNBALANCED, bid the other minor suit.

Then, show your MAXI HAND and your FIT by JUMP RAISING your partner's MINOR when it is your next turn to bid.

all the responses

When partner opens 1♣ or 1◇

MINI RESPONDING HAND **6 & 9** HCP

- 1ST → Bid a long suit, but not on the 2-level.
- 2ND → Bid 4-card suits up-the-ladder.
- 3RD → Bid 1NT. **LIMIT**
- 4TH → Raise partner's minor with 5 or more ♣s or ◇s.

MEDIUM RESPONDING HAND **10 & 12** HCP

- 1ST → Bid a long suit.
- 2ND → Bid 4-card suits up-the-ladder.
- 3RD → Bid 3 of partner's minor with 5 or more ♣s or ◇s.

MAXI RESPONDING HAND **13** or more HCP

- 1ST → Bid a long suit.
- 2ND → Bid 4-card suits up-the-ladder.
- 3RD → Bid 2NT.
- 4TH → Bid the other MINOR and then JUMP BID in partner's MINOR to show a FIT.

DON'T WORRY

About not making a LIMIT BID Right away. You can Always make a LIMIT BID When it's your next turn to bid.

OPENER WILL NOT PASS. If you don't make a limit bid, opener can't pass. You get another turn.

HOW TO DRAW A BRIDGE PLAYER

STEP ONE:

STEP TWO:

STEP THREE:

STEP FOUR:

CHANGING EXPRESSIONS:

CONCENTRATION   SURPRISE   GLEE

CHANGING POSITIONS:

SITTING BACK

HANDS IN POCKETS

LEANING FORWARD

CHANGING HAIR:

CHANGING HEADS:

FORCING BIDS

When 3 people pass in a row — PASS-PASS-PASS, remember, the bidding is OVER.

So, if you make a bid, then the person to your left passes, partner passes, and the opponent to your right passes - that makes 3 passes and the bidding is over.

This means you don't get another chance to bid!

Sometimes, you need to make more than one bid to tell partner about your hand. You don't want the bidding to be finished until you're finished!

If you need to make more than one bid to describe your hand

MAKE SURE YOUR FIRST BID IS FORCING!

FORCING BIDS SAY:

"Partner,— please make sure I get another chance to bid!"

If you make a **FORCING BID**, and the opponent to your left passes, your partner **MUST MAKE A BID**. If the opponent on your left makes a bid over your **FORCING BID**, then partner may pass if he wants because now you'll still get your other chance to bid!

Think about it —

If you bid, your left hand opponent bids, and now your partner passes, even if your right hand should pass, you get a bid —

BECAUSE there must be 3 passes before the bidding is over.

WHAT BIDS are FORCING?

THERE ARE EASY
RULES ABOUT
FORCING BIDS

☆☆ RULE ANY NON-LIMIT BID IS FORCING FOR ONE ROUND OF BIDDING.

Any time you make a bid that is not a limit bid, partner
MUST MAKE SURE YOU GET AT LEAST ONE MORE
CHANCE TO BID. Partner CANNOT allow the bidding
to be over before you get another chance to bid.
If you make a LIMIT BID, partner can add your points
to his and decide whether or not to let the bidding be over.

☆☆ RULE ANY JUMP BID IN A NEW SUIT IS FORCING TO GAME.

A JUMP BID is when you SKIP a WHOLE LEVEL.
If you make a JUMP bid in a new suit, partner CANNOT LET
THE BIDDING BE OVER UNTIL YOU BID A GAME. Partner
must keep the bidding going until you have bid to a game.

☆☆ RULE ☆ LIMIT BIDS ARE NOT FORCING. ☆ GAME BIDS ARE NOT FORCING.

WHAT ARE ROUNDS ?

Each time the bidding
goes all 'round the table is called a round. The first round is
the first time everyone gets a chance to bid. The second round
is the second chance to bid for each player. And so on. . . .

Review ALL RESPONSES TO 1♣/1◇

1. What are the 3 kinds of Responding Hands?
   a)_____ HCP_____
   b)_____ HCP_____
   c)_____ HCP_____

2. Partner opens 1♣ and you have a MINI hand. What are your 4 choices of response?
   a)_____
   b)_____
   c)_____
   d)_____

3. What are the two LIMIT BIDS you can make to show your MINI hand?
   a)_____
   b)_____

4. If partner opens 1♣ or 1◇ and you bid 1NT, what are you promising that you don't have.
   _____

5. Partner opens 1♣ or 1◇ and you have a MEDIUM hand. What are your 3 choices of response?
   a)_____
   b)_____
   c)_____

6. What is the LIMIT BID you can make to show your MEDIUM hand?
   _____

7. If partner opens 1♣ or 1◇ and you make a LIMIT BID what are you saying you DO NOT HAVE?
   _____

8. What is the RULE about LIMIT BIDS?_____

9. When partner opens 1 of a minor, your first job is to:
   _____
   _____

10. Partner opens 1♣ or 1◇ and you have a MAXI hand. What are your 4 main choices of response?

    a) _____

    b) _____

    c) _____

    d) _____

11. What bids are FORCING?

    a) _____

    b) _____

12. What bids are NOT FORCING?

    a) _____

    b) _____

13. What is a ROUND? _____

_____

_____

THE MAD NOTE TAKER

When Benjamin learns anything new, he takes LOTS OF NOTES. **try it!**
Copy these notes on a sheet of paper.
Then, study them. Give someone your notes. Get them to ask you questions and test your memory.

Responding to opening bids of 1♣, 1◇, 1♡, and 1♠.

MINI responding hands 6-9 HCP

1♡	2♡	LIMIT
	1♠	EXPLORE
	1NT	LIMIT
1♠	2♠	LIMIT
	1NT	LIMIT
1♣/1◇	LONG SUIT	EXPLORE
	4-CARD SUIT - UP-THE-LADDER	EXPLORE
	1NT LIMIT	
	2 OF OPENER'S MINOR	LIMIT

Medium responding hands 10-12 HCP

1♡/1♠	3♡/3♠	LIMIT
	LONG SUIT	EXPLORE
	4-CARD SUITS UP-THE-LADDER	EXPLORE
1♣/1◇	LONG SUIT	EXPLORE
	4-CARD SUITS UP-THE-LADDER	EXPLORE
	3 OF OPENER'S MINOR	LIMIT

Maxi responding hands 13+ HCP

1♡/1♠	4♡/4♠ GAME	LIMIT
	BID A LONG SUIT	EXPLORE
	4-CARD SUITS UP-THE-LADDER	EXPLORE
	2NT	GAME FORCE
1♣/1◇	BID A LONG SUIT	EXPLORE
	4-CARD SUITS	EXPLORE
	2NT GAME FORCE	

BID THE OTHER MINOR SUIT,
PLANNING TO BID OPENER'S MINOR SUIT
AT YOUR NEXT TURN TO BID

WHAT DO YOU KNOW ?

ABOUT RESPONSES TO 1 LEVEL OPENERS.

PART A. MINI RESPONDING HANDS (6-9 HCP)

YOUR HAND	OPENING BID	RESPONSE	LIMIT OR FORCING?
1. ♠ KJ106 ♥ A3 ♦ J752 ♣ 764	(1♠)	( )	_____
2. ♠ KJ106 ♥ A3 ♦ J752 ♣ 764	(1♥)	( )	_____
3. ♠ KJ106 ♥ A3 ♦ J752 ♣ 764	(1♣)	( )	_____
4. ♠ KJ10 ♥ A32 ♦ J752 ♣ 764	(1♦)	( )	_____
5. ♠ KJ10 ♥ A103 ♦ J752 ♣ 764	(1♣)	( )	_____
6. ♠ KJ106 ♥ A103 ♦ J75 ♣ 764	(1♥)	( )	_____

WHAT DO YOU KNOW ?

PART A (CONTINUED)

	YOUR HAND	OPENING BID	RESPONSE	LIMIT OR FORCING?
8.	♠ K 10 9 ♥ AQ 10 87 ♦ 10 83 ♣ 72	1♠		_____
8.	♠ K 10 ♥ AQ 10 87 ♦ 10 83 ♣ 10 7 2	1♠		_____
9.	♠ K 10 ♥ 10 9 ♦ AQ 10 832 ♣ 10 7 2	1♠		_____

PART B. MEDIUM RESPONDING HANDS (10-12 HCP)

	YOUR HAND	OPENING BID	RESPONSE	LIMIT OR FORCING?
1.	♠ AK 104 ♥ QJ 2 ♦ J 103 ♣ 764	1♠		_____
2.	♠ AK 104 ♥ QJ 2 ♦ J 103 ♣ 764	1♥		_____
3.	♠ AK 104 ♥ QJ 2 ♦ J 103 ♣ 764	1♣		_____
4.	♠ AJ 10 ♥ A 10 ♦ K 10 942 ♣ 943	1♣		_____

WHAT DO YOU KNOW ?

PART B (CONTINUED)

	YOUR HAND	OPENING BID	RESPONSE	LIMIT OR FORCING?
5.	♠ AJ10 ♡ A10 ♢ K10942 ♣ 942	(1♡)	( )	_____
6.	♠ AJ10 ♡ A109 ♢ K1094 ♣ 942	(1♣)	( )	_____
7.	♠ AJ103 ♡ A1094 ♢ Q1094 ♣ 9	(1♣)	( )	_____
8.	♠ AJ1032 ♡ A1094 ♢ Q1094 ♣ VOID	(1♣)	( )	_____
9.	♠ AJ ♡ A1094 ♢ Q1094 ♣ 983	(1♠)	( )	_____
10.	♠ AJ ♡ A10942 ♢ Q1094 ♣ 98	(1♠)	( )	_____

PART C. MAXI RESPONDING HANDS (13+ HCP)

1.	♠ AK104 ♡ QJ2 ♢ KJ10 ♣ 764			

WHAT DO YOU KNOW ?

PART C (CONTINUED)

	YOUR HAND	OPENING BID	RESPONSE	LIMIT OR FORCING?
2.	♠ AK104 ♡ QJ ♢ KJ10 ♣ 7642	1♡	◯	_____
3.	♠ AK10 ♡ QJ ♢ KJ103 ♣ 7642	1♡	◯	_____
4.	♠ AK ♡ QJ103 ♢ KJ103 ♣ 764	1♠	◯	_____
5.	♠ A10 ♡ AQJ103 ♢ K1032 ♣ 92	1♠	◯	_____
6.	♠ A1092 ♡ AQ ♢ K10932 ♣ 92	1♡	◯	_____
7.	♠ A109 ♡ A9 ♢ KJ1093 ♣ A92	1♢	◯	_____

WHAT DO YOU KNOW ?

PART C (CONTINUED)

YOUR HAND	OPENING BID	RESPONSE	LIMIT OR FORCING?
8. ♠ A109 ♡ A ◇ KJ1093 ♣ QJ93	(1◇)	( )	_____
9. ♠ A109 ♡ A9 ◇ KJ93 ♣ Q1092	(1♣)	( )	_____

PART D. MORE RESPONSES TO 1-LEVEL OPENINGS.

1. You open 1♡. What does partner mean by each of these responses:
   a) 2♡ _____
   b) 3♡ _____
   c) 1NT _____
   d) 2NT _____
   e) 4♡ _____

2. You open 1♣. What does partner mean by each of these responses:
   a) 1NT _____
   b) 1♠ _____
   c) 2NT _____
   d) 2♣ _____
   e) 3♣ _____

3. You open 1◇. As above, what does each response mean:
   a) 1♠ _____
   b) 2♣ _____
   c) 1NT _____
   d) 2◇ _____

4. You open 1♠. As above, what does each response mean:
   a) 3♠ _____
   b) 2♡ _____
   c) 4♠ _____
   d) 2♠ _____
   e) 1NT _____
   f) 2♣ _____

Partner Opens 1 No Trump (15 TO 17 HCP)

HOW TO RESPOND

WHEN PARTNER OPENS 1NT, YOU KNOW 3 THINGS:

☆ THE 1NT OPENING HAS 15, 16, OR 17 HCP.
☆ IT SHOWS NO 5-CARD OR LONGER MAJOR.
☆ IT IS BALANCED; REMEMBER THAT MEANS IT HAS NO SINGLETONS OR VOIDS, AND NO MORE THAN ONE DOUBLETON.

THE NO ZONE 7 HCP OR LESS

If you have LESS THAN 8 HCP you know there is no chance for GAME. Even if you have 7 HCP, add them to what partner has 7+15=22 , 7+16=23 , 7+17=24 no matter if partner had even 17 HCP, that's not enough for game. So, you'd like the bidding to be over soon. You can help do this in 2 ways.

PASS IF YOUR HAND IS **BALANCED.**

BID 2◇, 2♡, OR 2♠ IF YOU HAVE A **5-CARD SUIT OR LONGER.**

PARTNER WILL KNOW YOU WANT THE BIDDING TO BE OVER.

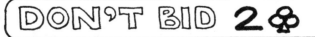

DON'T BID **2♣**

BECAUSE—
We are saving this bid.
It has a special meaning.
READ ON —
And learn your first CONVENTION!

Partner Opens 1 No Trump

HOW DO YOU RESPOND ?
The Invitation

If partner opens 1NT you know he has 15, 16, or 17 HCP.
BUT you don't know EXACTLY how many points, RIGHT ?
If you have 8 or 9 points, you want to bid to game if partner has 17 points but you don't want to bid to game if he has only 15 points. (If he has 16 points you might want to bid game if he has honor cards in each suit.)
BECAUSE 9 + 15 = Only 24 BUT 9 + 17 = 26 GAME !
You can ASK partner exactly how good the 1NT opener was by making:

An Invitation Bid

BID 2NT With a Balanced Hand
This says, "Partner, bid 3NT with 17 HCP, or 16 HCP and honor cards in each suit, or Pass with 15 HCP. I am inviting you to game."

BID 2♣ STAYMAN

HERE IT IS - JUST AS WE PROMISED - YOUR FIRST

CONVENTION

A CONVENTION

⇨ A CONVENTION IS A SPECIAL KIND OF BID.

⇨ CONVENTIONS ARE BIDS WITH SPECIAL MEANINGS.

⇨ CONVENTION BIDS USUALLY MEAN SOMETHING DIFFERENT FROM WHAT THEY SAY.

⇨ CONVENTION BIDS ARE NOT SAYING HOW MANY TRICKS YOU CAN WIN OR WHAT YOU WOULD LIKE TO BE TRUMP.

⇨ IN THE WORLD OF BRIDGE THERE ARE MANY, MANY CONVENTION BIDS.

⇨ IN THIS BOOK YOU WILL LEARN ONLY ONE OF THEM, BUT IT IS A VERY IMPORTANT ONE.

THIS CONVENTION IS CALLED:

STAYMAN

STAYMAN IS A RESPONSE OF

2♣ WHEN PARTNER OPENS 1NT.

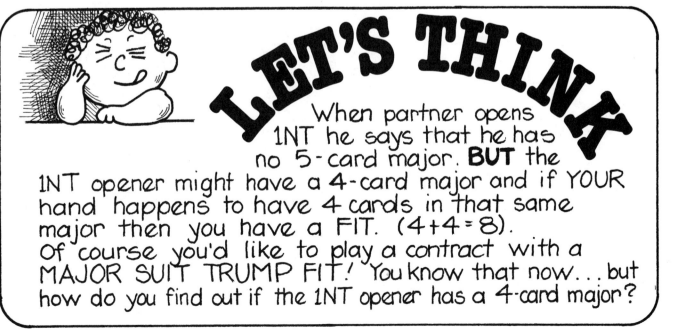

LET'S THINK

When partner opens 1NT he says that he has no 5-card major. **BUT** the 1NT opener might have a 4-card major and if YOUR hand happens to have 4 cards in that same major then you have a FIT. (4+4=8).

Of course you'd like to play a contract with a MAJOR SUIT TRUMP FIT! You know that now... but how do you find out if the 1NT opener has a 4-card major?

BID 2♣ STAYMAN

If partner opens 1NT and you respond 2♣,
you are asking this question:
"Partner - do you have a 4-card MAJOR?"

Now, partner will answer your question like this:

"2◇ - nope I don't"

Or

"2♡ - yup, I've got a 4-card ♡ suit"

Or

"2♠ - yup, I've got a 4-card ♠ suit, AND
I might have a 4-card ♡ suit, too!"

When opener has 2 4-card MAJORS, the bid
after 2♣ STAYMAN is 2♠.

If partner answers your STAYMAN QUESTION by
bidding 2 of YOUR major, you know you have a fit!

PARTNER BIDS 1NT
WHAT DO YOU RESPOND?

 The Invitation 8 OR 9 HCP - BID 2NT with a balanced hand and no 4-card or longer major.

BID STAYMAN

 IF PARTNER ANSWERS STAYMAN BY BIDDING YOUR SUIT- RAISE THE SUIT TO THE 3-LEVEL.

 O.K., PARD. We have a FIT. If you have 16 or 17 points, bid game. If you have only 15 points, please PASS.

 IF PARTNER ANSWERS STAYMAN BY NOT BIDDING YOUR SUIT.

BID 2NT if your suit was only 4-cards long.

BID Your major suit if it was 5-cards long.

BOTH OF THESE BIDS INVITE PARTNER TO GAME. If you have bid your major, you have shown 5 or more cards in that major. Now OPENER looks at his hand and asks:

 1. DO I HAVE A FIT?
2. DO I WANT TO BID GAME?

IF opener has a **FIT** but doesn't want to bid game, he PASSES.
IF opener has no **FIT** and doesn't want to bid game, he bids 2NT.

IF opener - has a **FIT** and wants to bid game, he bids 4♥ or 4♠.
IF opener has no **FIT** and wants to bid game, he bids 3NT.

The Invitation (8 OR 9 HCP)

PARTNER OPENS 1NT
AND YOU WANT TO INVITE OPENER TO GAME.

 2NT - balanced hand, no 4-card or longer major.

 2♣ STAYMAN with a 4- or 5-card major.

 LOOK!

Here is an example hand:

Opener	Responder
♠ A103	♠ J92
♡ KJ107	♡ A943
◇ A2	◇ K104
♣ KQ103	♣ J98

"1NT - I have 15-17 HCP with no 5-card major"   1st Round of bidding   "2♣ - do you have a 4-card major suit?"

"2♡ - yes, I do have a 4-card ♡ suit"   2nd Round of bidding   "3♡ - good! We have a fit. Do you want to bid game?"

"4♡ - YES! I have enough points for us to be in game!"   3rd Round of bidding   "Pass - what a wonderful partner"

124

BRIDGE ART

HOW WOULD YOU DRAW PEOPLE WHO ARE BIDDING?

We could draw it like this

Each time that the partners in the picture make a bid each, or two bids altogether, is ONE ROUND of bidding. These partners made 3 ROUNDS of bidding until they stopped, in game. Another way to show people bidding is like this

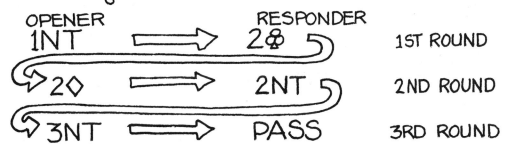

OPENER		RESPONDER	
1NT	⟹	2♣	1ST ROUND
2♦	⟹	2NT	2ND ROUND
3NT	⟹	PASS	3RD ROUND

That's easier to draw! But even quicker is to just put all of opener's bids in one column and all of responder's bids in another column:

EXAMPLE:

1NT	2♣
2♡	3♡
4♡	PASS

What was opener's 1st bid? _____
What was responder's 1st bid? _____
What was opener's 2nd bid? _____
How many rounds of bidding were there? _____
What is the final contract?

_____

EXAMPLE:

1NT	2♣
2♦	2♡
3NT	PASS

What was opener's 1st bid? _____
What was responder's 1st bid? _____
What was opener's 2nd bid? _____
How many rounds of bidding were there? _____
What is the final contract?

WHAT DO YOU KNOW ?

EXERCISE ON RESPONSES TO 1NT OPENINGS
HANDS IN THE 'NO ZONE' (less than 7 points) AND
INVITE HANDS (8-9 points)

Partner Opens 1 No Trump

	YOUR HAND	OPENER BIDS	YOU RESPOND	ANSWER
1.	♠ K 10 9 3 2 ♡ 5 ♢ 9862 ♣ 753	1NT	?	_____
2.	♠ K 9 3 ♡ A 4 2 ♢ 10832 ♣ 976	1NT	?	_____
3.	♠ 6543 ♡ KQJ8 ♢ Q32 ♣ 53	1NT	?	_____
4.	♠ A 10 9632 ♡ KQ10 ♢ 108 ♣ 32	1NT	?	_____
5.	♠ J 10 9 ♡ Q 10 8 ♢ AQ1093 ♣ 76	1NT	?	_____
6.	♠ 10 9 ♡ QJ1087 ♢ A 10 9 ♣ Q 10 9	1NT	?	_____

126

Partner Opens 1 No Trump

What is your STAYMAN Response?

In these questions, you will see your hand on the left and the bidding on the right. Look at the hand and think how you would respond to 1NT. Then look at the bidding. Follow the bidding and when you come to a question mark figure out the correct bid.

Look at this example:

YOUR HAND
- ♠ AK103
- ♡ Q1092
- ◇ 1098
- ♣ 76

OPENER	RESPONDER
1NT	2♣
2♡	?

ANSWER 3♡ INVITE

Now you try!

1.
- ♠ AK92
- ♡ 1092
- ◇ Q1098
- ♣ 76

OPENER	RESPONDER
1NT	2♣
2♡	?

ANSWER _____

2.
- ♠ Q103
- ♡ AJ92
- ◇ J103
- ♣ 972

1NT	2♣
2♠	?

ANSWER _____

3.
- ♠ AK1092
- ♡ 109
- ◇ Q1098
- ♣ 76

1NT	2♣
2♡	?

ANSWER _____

4.
- ♠ Q103
- ♡ AJ92
- ◇ J103
- ♣ 972

1NT	2♣
2◇	?

ANSWER _____

THE WHOLE HAND

You know lots about bridge now. We think you should be able to look at a picture or diagram of all 52 cards and not be confused. In the diagrams below, look at the hands, see who starts the bidding (dealer) and fill in all the bids. Decide what YOU would bid with each hand.
(This is how puzzles are drawn in grown-ups' bridge books!)

1.

```
              ♠ 65432
              ♥ KQJ8
              ◇ Q3
              ♣ 53
   ♠ 987         N        ♠ QJ10
   ♥ 42                   ♥ 1076
   ◇ K876    W      E     ◇ J952
   ♣ J1074               ♣ AK2
                 S
              ♠ AK
              ♥ A953
              ◇ A104
              ♣ Q986
```

DEALER: NORTH   BIDDING:

N	E	S	W
___	___	___	___
___	___	___	___
___	___	___	___
___	___	___	___

FINAL CONTRACT: _____

3.

```
              ♠ KQJ73
              ♥ 852
              ◇ K106
              ♣ 73
   ♠ A84         N        ♠ 106
   ♥ AQJ                  ♥ K963
   ◇ AQ7     W      E     ◇ 943
   ♣ 10852               ♣ AQJ6
                 S
              ♠ 952
              ♥ 1074
              ◇ J852
              ♣ K94
```

DEALER: EAST   BIDDING:

N	E	S	W
___	___	___	___
___	___	___	___
___	___	___	___
___	___	___	___

FINAL CONTRACT: _____

2.

```
              ♠ AKQ
              ♥ K109
              ◇ 9852
              ♣ A52
   ♠ J10962       N        ♠ 74
   ♥ Q86532                ♥ 4
   ◇ VOID    W      E     ◇ KQJ1063
   ♣ Q8                  ♣ 10974
                 S
              ♠ 853
              ♥ AJ7
              ◇ A74
              ♣ KJ63
```

DEALER: WEST   BIDDING:

N	E	S	W
___	___	___	___
___	___	___	___
___	___	___	___
___	___	___	___

FINAL CONTRACT: _____

4.

```
              ♠ 65
              ♥ QJ76
              ◇ J765
              ♣ 876
   ♠ AK3          N        ♠ QJ874
   ♥ A9                    ♥ 83
   ◇ Q1042   W      E     ◇ A98
   ♣ A1093               ♣ Q54
                 S
              ♠ 1092
              ♥ K10542
              ◇ K3
              ♣ KJ2
```

DEALER: SOUTH   BIDDING:

N	E	S	W
___	___	___	___
___	___	___	___
___	___	___	___
___	___	___	___

FINAL CONTRACT: _____

Partner Opens 1 No Trump

HOW DO YOU RESPOND?

If partner opens 1NT, you know there are 15-17 points across from you. If you have 10 HCP or more, you two have enough HCP for game.

 BID 3NT WITH A BALANCED HAND AND NO 4-CARD OR LONGER MAJOR.

 BID A 5-CARD SUIT ON THE 3-LEVEL
This 3♣, 3♦, 3♥ or 3♠ bid by you is FORCING. You are showing partner you have a 5-card suit and are looking for a FIT.
OPENER MUST now bid game, so even if he doesn't have a FIT, he will bid 3NT.

 BID 2♣ STAYMAN

① IF YOU FIND A **FIT**, RAISE TO GAME.

② IF YOU HAVE **NO FIT** ⇨ BID 3NT.

  **GAME FORCE** RESPONSES AFTER 1NT OPENER

(10 HCP or MORE)

➡ (**BID 4♡ OR 4♠** If you have 6 or more.)

YOU KNOW YOU HAVE A FIT BECAUSE PARTNER HAS AT LEAST 2 OF YOUR SUIT.

➡ (**BID 5♣ OR 5♢** IF YOU HAVE 6 OR MORE AND A SINGLETON OR VOID.)

BE SURE YOU WANT TO PLAY IN 5♣ OR 5♢, INSTEAD OF 3NT! WITH NO SINGLETON OR VOID YOU MAY WANT TO BID 3NT. IF YOU HAVE A VOID OR A SINGLETON, YOU'LL WANT TO BE IN 5♣ OR 5♢.

THE GAME FORCE (10 OR MORE HCP) RESPONSES TO 1NT OPENINGS

➡ (**BID 3NT** BALANCED HAND, NO 4-CARD OR LONGER MAJOR. PARTNER IS <u>NOT</u> FORCED TO BID– 3NT <u>IS</u> GAME!)

➡ (**BID** A 5-CARD SUIT AT THE 3-LEVEL. THE 1NT OPENER MUST BID.)

➡ (**BID 2♣ STAYMAN** 1NT OPENER <u>MUST</u> BID!)

AFTER STAYMAN: ① IF YOU FIND A FIT, RAISE TO GAME.
② WITH NO FIT, BID 3NT.

➡ (**BID 4♡ OR 4♠** IF YOU HAVE 6 OR MORE.)

➡ (**BID 5♣ OR 5♢** IF YOU HAVE 6 OR MORE. AND A SINGLETON OR VOID.)

WHAT DO YOU KNOW ?

Exercise on RESPONSES to 1NT with a GAME FORCE
HAND (10 + points)

YOUR HAND:	OPENER BIDS	YOU RESPOND	ANSWER
1. ♠ AK10 ♡ Q93 ♢ QJ10 ♣ 10932	1NT	?	_____
2. ♠ AK109 ♡ Q93 ♢ QJ10 ♣ 1093	1NT	?	_____
3. ♠ A109 ♡ KQ9362 ♢ QJ10 ♣ 3	1NT	?	_____
4. ♠ A109 ♡ 9 ♢ QJ10 ♣ KQ9632	1NT	?	_____
5. ♠ AK109 ♡ Q93 ♢ QJ109 ♣ 63	1NT 2♠	2♣ ?	_____
6. ♠ AK109 ♡ Q93 ♢ QJ109 ♣ 63	1NT 2♢	2♣ ?	_____
7. ♠ AK1092 ♡ Q93 ♢ QJ109 ♣ 3	1NT	?	_____

131

SLAM ZONE

DO YOU REMEMBER WHEN WE TALKED ABOUT SLAMS?

small slam 6♣ 6♦ 6♥ 6♠ 6NT
12 TRICKS

7NT 7♦ 7♣ 7♠ 7♥ *grand slam*
13 TRICKS

Let's talk about these a bit.
Can you guess how many points you and partner
need to make a slam?
If you just guessed lots of points,
you are right!

There 40 points in the whole deck.
You and partner need at least 33 of these
points to even THINK about bidding a SLAM.

33-36 POINTS IS USUALLY ENOUGH FOR A SMALL SLAM

37-40 POINTS IS ENOUGH FOR A GRAND SLAM

If you remember these two POINT RANGES
you'll know when you should
TRY FOR SLAM.

Partner Opens 1 No Trump

(15 TO 17 HCP)

HOW TO RESPOND IN
THE SLAM ZONE

If you have 16 or more points, and PARTNER opens 1NT, you know that your team is in the SLAM ZONE.

➡ ## WITH A BALANCED HAND
AND NO 5 OR 6-CARD SUITS
AND NO 4-CARD MAJOR
AND NO SINGLETONS OR VOIDS

☆ 16 or 17 HCP ◆ RESPOND 4NT
☆ 18 or 19 HCP ◆ RESPOND 6NT
☆ 20 or 21 HCP ◆ RESPOND 5NT
☆ 22 or MORE HCP ◆ BID 7NT

THE 4NT RESPONSE IS A

LIMIT BID

Opener can add his points to yours and decide if he should bid more or PASS. The 5NT response is FORCING, opener must either bid 6NT or 7NT.

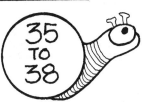

15 TO 17 + 16 OR 17 = 31 TO 34

15 TO 17 + 18 TO 19 = 33 TO 36

15 TO 17 + 20 TO 21 = 35 TO 38

15 TO 17 + 22 OR MORE = 37 OR MORE

133

Partner Opens 1 No Trump

(15 to 17 HCP)

HOW TO RESPOND IN
THE SLAM ZONE

➡️ **WITH AN UNBALANCED HAND**

☆ WITH A 6-CARD (OR LONGER) SUIT.
YOU KNOW YOU HAVE A FIT, RIGHT?

➡️ BID 5 of your suit with 15-17 points.
➡️ BID 6 of your suit with 18-21 points.
➡️ BID 7 of your suit with 22 or more points.

☆ WITH A 5-CARD SUIT
BID LIKE YOU WOULD WITH A GAME FORCE HAND.

➡️ BID 3 OF YOUR SUIT and EXPLORE.

☆ If partner shows a FIT, RAISE the suit
way up: TO THE 5-LEVEL WITH 15-17 POINTS
TO THE 6-LEVEL WITH 18-21 POINTS
TO THE 7-LEVEL WITH 22 OR MORE POINTS

☆ If partner doesn't raise your suit,
BID NT way up.

| 4NT | 16-17 | 5NT | 20-21 |
| 6NT | 18-19 | 7NT | 22 OR MORE |

☆ WITH A 4-CARD MAJOR
➡️ BID 2♣ STAYMAN and EXPLORE.

☆ If partner shows a fit now RAISE it like before.

☆ If partner doesn't show a fit, BID
NO TRUMP like before.

WHAT DO YOU KNOW ?

Exercise on RESPONSES to 1NT with SLAM HANDS.

YOUR HAND:	OPENER BIDS	YOU RESPOND	ANSWER

1. ♠ AK10
   ♡ QJ9
   ◇ A103
   ♣ QJ98

   1NT   ?   _____

2. ♠ AK10
   ♡ QJ98
   ◇ A103
   ♣ QJ9

   1NT   ?   _____

3. ♠ AK10
   ♡ QJ98
   ◇ A103
   ♣ QJ9

   1NT   2♣
   2♡   ?   _____

4. ♠ AK10
   ♡ QJ98
   ◇ A103
   ♣ QJ9

   1NT   2♣
   2♠   ?   _____

5. ♠ AKJ1093
   ♡ 9
   ◇ AQ10
   ♣ A92

   1NT   ?   _____

6. ♠ AKJ109
   ♡ 93
   ◇ AQ10
   ♣ A92

   1NT   ?   _____

7. ♠ AKJ109
   ♡ 93
   ◇ AQ10
   ♣ A92

   1NT   3♠
   3NT   ?   _____

all the responses
TO AN OPENING BID OF 1NT

NO ZONE 0-7 HCP	◆ PASS ◆ 2◇, 2♡, 2♠ with a 5-card or longer suit.

INVITATION 8 or 9 HCP	◆ 2NT with a balanced hand and no MAJOR suit. ◆ 2♣ STAYMAN with a 4-card or longer MAJOR suit.

GAME FORCE
10 to 15
HCP
	◆ 3♣, 3◇, 3♡, or 3♠ with a 5-card suit. FORCING.
	◆ 3NT with a balanced hand.
	◆ 2♣ STAYMAN with a 4-card
	    MAJOR
	◆ 4♡ or 4♠ with a 6-card or longer suit.
	◆ 5♣ or 5◇ with a 6-card or longer suit
	    and a singleton or void.

SLAM ZONE 16 OR MORE HCP	◆ BALANCED HAND	4NT	15-17 HCP
		6NT	18-19 HCP
		5NT	20-21 HCP
		7NT	22 + HCP
	◆ 6-card or longer SUIT	5-level	15-17 HCP
		6-level	18-21 HCP
		7-level	22+ HCP
	◆ STAYMAN with other hands looking for a fit. Then bid as above.		

A NOTE from your TEACHERS

Responding to 1NT openings may seem
a bit tough, but it is VERY IMPORTANT.
Try to learn them as best you can,
and always keep this book around to look
up things in when you get stumped!

Review

You have learned a lot in PART TWO— all about Responding! Before we move on to PART THREE, here are some exercises to do. Test yourself! If you don't do as well as you think you should, go back and read PART TWO again. Do this test in PENCIL! Then you can erase any answers you might have got wrong, and do the test again after re-reading PART TWO.

RESPONDING WITH A MINI HAND (6-9 HCP)

YOUR HAND:	OPENER BIDS	YOU RESPOND	ANSWER
1. ♠ J843 ♡ J5 ◇ QJ98 ♣ Q85	1♠	?	_____
2. ♠ 10852 ♡ K54 ◇ A102 ♣ J95	1♣	?	_____
3. ♠ KJ9 ♡ J109 ◇ Q1093 ♣ Q109	1◇	?	_____
4. ♠ Q1032 ♡ J1092 ◇ AQ3 ♣ 102	1♣	?	_____
5. ♠ KJ952 ♡ QJ103 ◇ Q102 ♣ 2	1♣	?	_____
6. ♠ KJ952 ♡ QJ10 ◇ Q10 ♣ 1093	1♡	?	_____

Review

YOUR HAND:	OPENER BIDS	YOU RESPOND	ANSWER
7. ♠ A8 ♡ QJ10 ♢ Q10932 ♣ 1076	1♠	?	_____
8. ♠ AK103 ♡ 432 ♢ J1092 ♣ 107	1♣	?	_____

RESPONDING WITH A MEDIUM HAND (10-12 HCP)

YOUR HAND:	OPENER BIDS	YOU RESPOND	ANSWER
1. ♠ A109 ♡ QJ7 ♢ A932 ♣ 1093	1♡	?	_____
2. ♠ A10 ♡ QJ76 ♢ A932 ♣ 1093	1♠	?	_____
3. ♠ KJ10 ♡ Q10 ♢ AQ932 ♣ 1098	1♡	?	_____
4. ♠ AQ10 ♡ Q10 ♢ A932 ♣ 5432	1♡	?	_____
5. ♠ 10932 ♡ QJ10 ♢ A93 ♣ A109	1♣	?	_____

Review RESPONDING WITH A MEDIUM HAND (10-12 HCP), CONTINUED.

YOUR HAND:	OPENER BIDS	YOU RESPOND	ANSWER
6. ♠ QJ10 ♡ A1093 ♢ 5432 ♣ A10	1♡	?	_____
7. ♠ A10 ♡ QJ9832 ♢ K109 ♣ 72	1♣	?	_____
8. ♠ KQ7 ♡ QJ9 ♢ K109 ♣ 10862	1♠	?	_____
9. ♠ AK102 ♡ 432 ♢ QJ9 ♣ Q109	1♡	?	_____
10. ♠ A10 ♡ J10932 ♢ AK98 ♣ 92	1♣	?	_____

RESPONDING WITH A MAXI HAND (13+HCP)

1. ♠ AK10 ♡ Q1092 ♢ KJ109 ♣ 87	1♠	?	_____
2. ♠ A109 ♡ KQ1092 ♢ KJ10 ♣ 87	1♣	?	_____

Review RESPONDING WITH A MAXI HAND (13+ HCP), CONTINUED.

YOUR HAND:	OPENER BIDS	YOU RESPOND	ANSWER
3. ♠ A109 ♡ KQ109 ◇ KJ102 ♣ 87	1♣	?	_____
4. ♠ A109 ♡ KQ10 ◇ KJ9 ♣ 10987	1♣	?	_____
5. ♠ KJ109 ♡ Q10 ◇ AK32 ♣ Q103	1♡	?	_____
6. ♠ AK9 ♡ Q10 ◇ KJ1093 ♣ Q32	1♡	?	_____
7. ♠ AKQ10 ♡ KJ103 ◇ A92 ♣ AK	1♣	?	_____
8. ♠ AJ ♡ QJ108 ◇ KJ93 ♣ K109	1♠	?	_____
9. ♠ QJ109 ♡ 432 ◇ AK9 ♣ KJ10	1♡	?	_____

Review
RESPONDING WITH A MAXI HAND (13+ HCP), CONTINUED.

YOUR HAND	OPENER BIDS	YOU RESPOND	ANSWER
10. ♠ K10 ♡ A9 ◇ Q1087 ♣ AK1093	1♣	?	_____

RESPONDING TO 1NT OPENINGS

1. ♠ 109 ♡ A103 ◇ Q9862 ♣ 732	1NT	?	_____
2. ♠ J109 ♡ A1032 ◇ Q98 ♣ 732	1NT	?	_____
3. ♠ AJ109 ♡ A1032 ◇ 109 ♣ 732	1NT	?	_____
4. ♠ AJ ♡ 1032 ◇ A10983 ♣ 732	1NT	?	_____
5. ♠ J10 ♡ AQ10932 ◇ 76 ♣ K103	1NT	?	_____
6. ♠ A103 ♡ QJ9 ◇ Q1093 ♣ 732	1NT	?	_____

Review RESPONDING TO 1 NO TRUMP OPENINGS, CONTINUED.

YOUR HAND	OPENER BIDS	YOU RESPOND	ANSWER
7. ♠ AJ ♡ AQ10932 ♢ 76 ♣ K103	1NT	?	_____
8. ♠ A1093 ♡ QJ86 ♢ A2 ♣ K109	1NT 2♢	2♣ ?	_____
9. ♠ A10932 ♡ QJ8 ♢ A2 ♣ K103	1NT	?	_____
10. ♠ KQJ9 ♡ A32 ♢ K1032 ♣ 76	1NT 2♠	2♣ ?	_____
11. ♠ AK103 ♡ Q1092 ♢ A10 ♣ A98	1NT 2♢	2♣ ?	_____
12. ♠ AK1032 ♡ Q109 ♢ K108 ♣ A9	1NT 3NT	3♠ ?	_____
13. ♠ AK1032 ♡ Q109 ♢ K108 ♣ A9	1NT 4♠	3♠ ?	_____

Review
RESPONDING TO 1 NO TRUMP OPENINGS, CONTINUED.

YOUR HAND	OPENER BIDS	YOU RESPOND	ANSWER
14. ♠ QJ10 ♡ AK9 ♢ A1087 ♣ Q109	1NT	?	_____
15. ♠ A109 ♡ Q85 ♢ AKJ1032 ♣ 3	1NT	?	_____

NOW, CHECK YOUR ANSWERS.

HOW DID YOU DO ?

THIS HAS BEEN A LOT OF WORK!

YOU DESERVE A BREAK - TAKE ONE!

WHAT'S NEXT ?

More on bidding...

part three

THE BIDDING

After the first couple of bids you and partner have made, you should have a good idea about each other's hands.

Sometimes, you'll find a fit, but won't have enough points for game,
so you'll stop bidding at the 2- or 3-level.

And sometimes you'll have enough points for game and you'll bid it.

Or, you'll have lots of points to bid right up to a slam!

think & remember The bids you make are telling partner about your hand.
Partner's bids tell about his hand. **listen**

always ··· Think of your partner's hand as it fits with your hand.

always ··· Add the 2 hands together.

always ···

Try to find your MAJOR SUIT FIT.

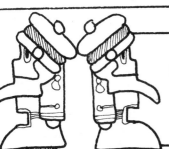

 **♣REMEMBER♣**
LIMIT BIDS!

It's a good idea to make a LIMIT BID so partner knows how high to bid.

CITY LIMITS

OPENER'S REBID

AFTER OPENING AND HEARING PARTNER'S RESPONSE, OPENER CAN TAKE A NEW LOOK AT THE HAND. IF RESPONDER HAS MADE A **LIMIT BID**, OPENER KNOWS WHAT CONTRACT TO PLAY.

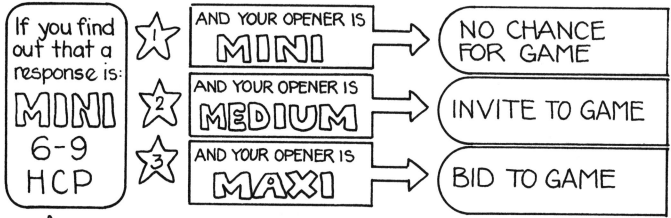

If you find out that a response is: MINI 6-9 HCP

⭐1 AND YOUR OPENER IS MINI → NO CHANCE FOR GAME

⭐2 AND YOUR OPENER IS MEDIUM → INVITE TO GAME

⭐3 AND YOUR OPENER IS MAXI → BID TO GAME

⭐ If responder's hand is MINI (6-9) and opener's hand is MINI (13-14), they will never add up to enough points for game.

⭐ If responder's hand is MINI (6-9) and opener's hand is MEDIUM (15-17), they might add up to GAME, when responder has 8 or 9 points and opener has 16 or 17 points. When this happens, you'll need to ask by INVITING GAME, once you have a FIT or in NO TRUMP.

⭐ If responder's hand is MINI (6-9) and opener's hand is MAXI (18-21), you know GAME is very likely so you must BID GAME. If you have found a fit, you can bid game in that suit. If you don't have a FIT, you can bid GAME in NO TRUMP.

MINI + MINI = NO CHANCE FOR GAME
MINI + MEDIUM = INVITE TO GAME
MINI + MAXI = BID GAME

OPENER'S REBIDS

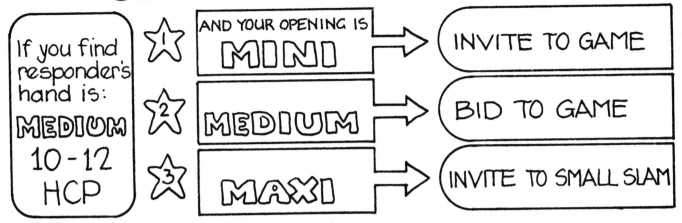

If you find responder's hand is: **MEDIUM** 10-12 HCP

⭐1 AND YOUR OPENING IS **MINI** → INVITE TO GAME

⭐2 **MEDIUM** → BID TO GAME

⭐3 **MAXI** → INVITE TO SMALL SLAM

⭐1 If RESPONDER'S hand is MEDIUM (10-12), and OPENER'S hand is WEAK (13-14), the two hands may add up to enough for GAME. In this case, you would ask by inviting to GAME.

⭐2 If RESPONDER'S hand is MEDIUM (10-12), and OPENER'S hand is MEDIUM (15-17), the two hands add up to enough points for GAME. You must bid game. If you find a fit, you can bid game in that suit. If not, you can bid GAME in NO TRUMP.

⭐3 If RESPONDER'S hand is MEDIUM (10-12), and OPENER'S hand is STRONG (18-21), the two hands might add up to enough for a SMALL SLAM. To find out, you will need to ask by INVITING SLAM.

MEDIUM + MINI = INVITE TO GAME
MEDIUM + MEDIUM = BID TO GAME
MEDIUM + MAXI = INVITE TO SLAM

OPENER'S REBIDS

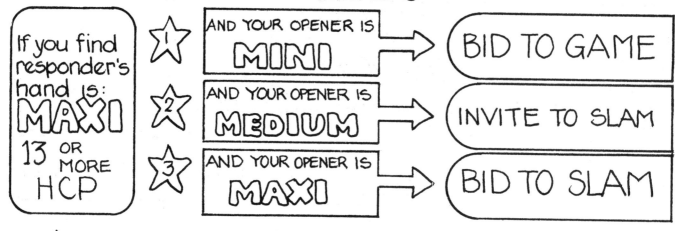

If you find responder's hand is: **MAXI** 13 OR MORE HCP

☆ 1	AND YOUR OPENER IS **MINI**	→	BID TO GAME
☆ 2	AND YOUR OPENER IS **MEDIUM**	→	INVITE TO SLAM
☆ 3	AND YOUR OPENER IS **MAXI**	→	BID TO SLAM

☆1 If RESPONDER'S hand is MAXI and OPENER'S hand is MINI, you know there are enough points for GAME, you must bid to GAME.

☆2 If RESPONDER'S hand is MAXI and OPENER'S hand is MEDIUM, you know there are more than enough points for game. You should INVITE to SLAM.

☆3 If RESPONDER'S hand is MAXI, (remember 13+ points) and OPENER'S hand is MAXI. You know you have enough points for SLAM. You should bid SLAM. You and partner might even get to a GRAND SLAM.

MAXI + MINI = BID TO GAME
MAXI + MEDIUM = INVITE TO SLAM
MAXI + MAXI = BID TO SLAM

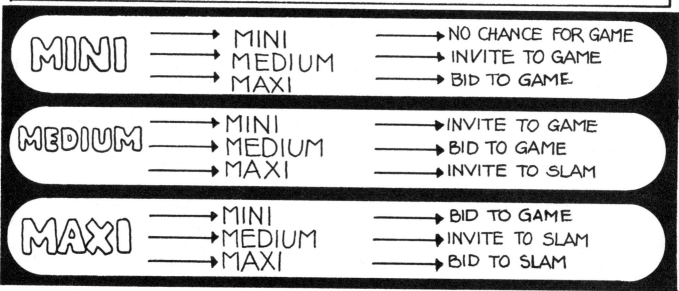

MINI	→ MINI	→ NO CHANCE FOR GAME
	→ MEDIUM	→ INVITE TO GAME
	→ MAXI	→ BID TO GAME

MEDIUM	→ MINI	→ INVITE TO GAME
	→ MEDIUM	→ BID TO GAME
	→ MAXI	→ INVITE TO SLAM

MAXI	→ MINI	→ BID TO GAME
	→ MEDIUM	→ INVITE TO SLAM
	→ MAXI	→ BID TO SLAM

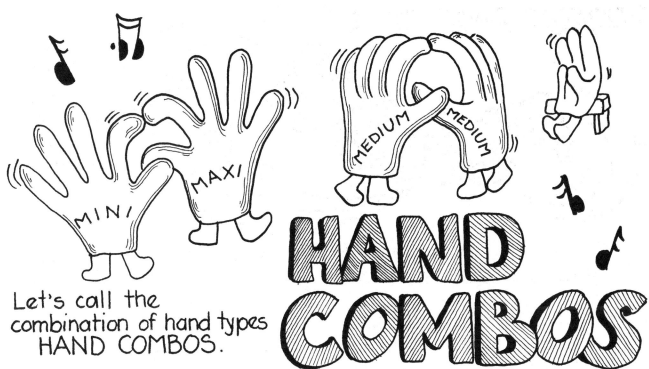

Let's call the combination of hand types HAND COMBOS.

HAND COMBOS

DO YOU REMEMBER ALL THE POSSIBLE COMBOS?

MINI ▭ MINI   MEDIUM ▭ MEDIUM
MINI ▭ MEDIUM   MEDIUM ▭ MAXI
MINI ▭ MAXI   MAXI ▭ MAXI

You don't have to worry who's got what. These COMBOS work the same for OPENER and RESPONDER.

When you make a LIMIT BID, you are telling partner what kind of hand you have. Now partner can tell what kind of HAND COMBO you have together.

When partner makes a LIMIT BID, that bid tells you what kind of hand partner has. Now you can figure out what HAND COMBO your team has.

ONCE YOU OR PARTNER FIND YOUR **HAND COMBO** YOU OR PARTNER CAN:
1. PASS BELOW GAME
2. INVITE GAME
3. BID GAME
4. INVITE SLAM
5. BID SLAM

FLASH CARDS

One really good idea for helping you to remember HAND COMBOS is to make some FLASH CARDS.

WHAT YOU WILL NEED:
- some blank cards, like recipe or index cards.
- a felt pen

ALL YOU DO: copy the COMBOS on one side and how you should bid on the other side.

FRONTS								
MINI + MINI	MINI + MEDIUM	MINI + MAXI	MEDIUM + MINI	MEDIUM + MEDIUM	MEDIUM + MAXI	MAXI + MINI	MAXI + MEDIUM	MAXI + MAXI

BACKS								
NO CHANCE FOR GAME	INVITE TO GAME	BID GAME	INVITE TO GAME	BID GAME	INVITE TO SLAM	BID GAME	INVITE TO SLAM	BID SLAM

NOW: FIND SOMEONE TO FLASH THEM FOR YOU!

MAXI + MINI

LIMIT BIDS

If responder didn't LIMIT his hand, it is up to you
to LIMIT your hand if you can.
This way your partner will know how high to bid.

HERE ARE SOME LIMIT BIDS YOU CAN MAKE:

MINI OPENING HANDS  13 OR 14 HCP

REBIDS

➤ **REBID NT WITHOUT A JUMP**

If you bid 1NT as your 2nd bid
(your REBID), you are showing a MINI
OPENING HAND, but NOT a 15-17 point
hand, as if you opened 1NT.

➤ **RAISE PARTNER'S SUIT**

If you raise partner's suit one level
you are promising at least 4 cards
in that suit, but only 13-14 points.

REBIDS

➤ **REBID YOUR MAJOR SUIT**

If you opened 1♡ or 1♠ you showed 5
or more, bid ♡s or ♠s again, to show 6+.

➤ **REBID YOUR MINOR SUIT**

If you opened 1♣ or 1◇ you showed
only 3 of them. You can REBID them
to show you had 5 or more.

LIMIT **ANY** OF THESE REBIDS
ARE LIMIT BIDS
AND SHOW 13-14 HCP.

LIMIT BIDS

MEDIUM OPENING HAND (15 TO 17 HCP)

There aren't as many LIMIT BIDS for a MEDIUM OPENING HAND. Most of the time you will be making FORCING BIDS until you discover what kind of hand RESPONDER has.

 If responder bid 1NT, **RAISE TO 2NT**.

 If responder bid 2 of your major, raise to 3 of the major.

 If responder bid a new suit, and you have a FIT, **JUMP RAISE** that new suit.

MAXI OPENING HAND (18 TO 21 HCP)

 If responder bid 1NT, **RAISE TO 3NT**.

 If responder bid 2 of your major, **RAISE TO GAME**.

 IF RESPONDER BID A NEW SUIT AND YOU HAVE A FIT FOR THE NEW SUIT, **RAISE TO GAME**.

 If you have a balanced hand, **JUMP BID IN NT**.

⭐ IF YOU OPEN 1♣ OR 1♦ AND JUMP BID IN **NT** NEXT BID, YOU SHOW 18-21 HCP.

❧REMEMBER❧ If you are wondering what your 2nd bid should be, **think** .

Did partner make a LIMIT BID? If so, you can decide what to do by remembering the HAND COMBOS you learned.

The Invitations

IF RESPONDER'S HAND IS LIMITED AND OPENER WANTS TO MAKE AN INVITE BID or IF OPENER'S HAND IS LIMITED AND RESPONDER WANTS TO MAKE AN INVITE BID:

remember THE HAND COMBINATIONS
MINI + MEDIUM = INVITE TO GAME
MEDIUM + MAXI = INVITE TO SLAM

HERE IS HOW YOU DO IT!

➡ IF YOU HAVE FOUND A FIT
RAISE THAT SUIT TO THE THREE LEVEL.

 IF YOU ARE INVITING TO GAME
* RAISE ♡S TO 3♡
* RAISE ♠S TO 3♠
* RAISE ♣S TO 3♣
* RAISE ♢S TO 3♢

➡ IF YOUR PARTNER BID NO TRUMP
RAISE TO 2NT TO INVITE TO GAME
RAISE TO 5NT TO INVITE TO SLAM

THE FIT

IF YOU HAVE FOUND A FIT...

ONCE YOU HAVE FOUND A **FIT**
IT IS EASY TO MAKE A **LIMIT BID**
SO PARTNER KNOWS WHAT CONTRACT TO PLAY.

OPENER

WITH A MINI – RAISES THE SUIT OF FIT ONE LEVEL.

WITH A MEDIUM – RAISES THE SUIT OF FIT TWO LEVELS.

WITH A MAXI – RAISES THE SUIT OF FIT TO GAME.

RESPONDER

WITH A MINI – RAISES THE SUIT OF FIT TO THE 2-LEVEL.

WITH A MEDIUM – RAISES THE SUIT OF FIT TO THE 3-LEVEL.

WITH A MAXI – RAISES THE SUIT OF FIT TO GAME.

IF YOU HAVEN'T FOUND A FIT

EXPLORE

BID UP-THE-LADDER

IF YOU DON'T HAVE A LONG SUIT
YOU MUST BID 4-CARD SUITS
UP-THE-LADDER. THIS WILL HELP
TO FIND **THE FIT** AS SOON AS POSSIBLE
SO YOU OR PARTNER CAN **LIMIT**
YOUR HAND. HERE ARE SOME EXAMPLES:

OPENER	RESPONDER
1♣	1♥
1♠	3♠ A FIT!

OPENER	RESPONDER
1♣	1◇
1♥	1♠
2♠ A FIT!	

OPENER	RESPONDER
1◇	1♥
3♥ A FIT!	

OPENER	RESPONDER
1♣	1♥
1♠	NO FIT! 1NT

If you ever
bid the same suit again
(REBID the same suit),
you are promising

1 MORE CARD

in that suit than you promised the last time
you bid it.
   If the first time you responded ♤s you promised
      only 4, when you bid ♤s again you
         are showing 5 ♤,
         if you bid ♤s again
         you are showing 6, and so on.

If you opened 1♡
   you promised 5♡s
   If you bid ♡s again you are promising 6.
   remember
YOU CAN ALWAYS HAVE **MORE** CARDS IN A SUIT
THAN YOU PROMISED,
BUT YOU SHOULD **NEVER** HAVE LESS.

   BIDDING
   should keep on going
      until either OPENER or RESPONDER
   has limited his hand,
OR until you have reached
a GAME or SLAM.

TEST YOURSELF

1. What is a rebid? _____
_____

2. If responder has LIMITED his hand by making
   a LIMIT BID, you can look at your hand and know
   how high to bid. Fill in the HAND COMBOS below.
   a) MINI + MINI ———————> _____
   b) MINI + MEDIUM ———————> _____
   c) MINI + MAXI ———————> _____
   d) MEDIUM + MINI ———————> _____
   e) MEDIUM + MEDIUM ———————> _____
   f) MEDIUM + MAXI ———————> _____
   g) MAXI + MINI ———————> _____
   h) MAXI + MEDIUM ———————> _____
   i) MAXI + MAXI ———————> _____

3. If responder has NOT LIMITED his hand by making
   a LIMIT bid, OPENER must try to LIMIT the OPENING
   hand. NOW, RESPONDER can tell what HAND COMBO
   your team has.
   WRITE THE 4 WAYS TO LIMIT A MINI OPENING HAND.
   a) _____
   b) _____
   c) _____
   d) _____
   WRITE THE 3 WAYS TO LIMIT A MEDIUM OPENING HAND.
   a) _____
   b) _____
   c) _____
   WRITE THE 4 WAYS TO LIMIT A MAXI OPENING HAND.
   a) _____
   b) _____
   c) _____
   d) _____

THERE'S MORE

TEST YOURSELF

4. If RESPONDER or OPENER has LIMITED his hand, and partner wants to make an INVITE bid, how would YOU do it?

   a) IF YOU HAVE A FIT _____

   _____

   b) IN NO TRUMP _____

   _____

5. What are the 2 HAND COMBOS that you will INVITE with?

   a) _____ + _____ INVITE TO _____

   b) _____ + _____ INVITE TO _____

6. When you find a FIT it is easy to make a LIMIT BID, to help partner know what contract to play. What is the FIT-SHOWING LIMIT BID with each of the 3 kinds of opening hand?

   a) MINI _____

   b) MEDIUM _____

   c) MAXI _____

And what is the FIT-SHOWING LIMIT BID with each of the 3 kinds of responding hand?

   a) MINI _____

   b) MEDIUM _____

   c) MAXI _____

7. If you haven't found a FIT, you want to EXPLORE, if you can. How do you do this?

   _____

   _____

8. If you ever bid your own suit again (REBID), what are you saying?

   _____

   _____

9. Bidding should keep on going until: _____

   _____

Review

Here are some bridge bidding quizzes. Questions are on the left, answers on the right. Cover the answers, and work out the correct bid by yourself. If you get the answer right, put a check mark by the question. If you were wrong, leave the question, and go back to it later.

YOUR HAND:	YOU BID	PARTNER BIDS	ANSWER
1. ♠ K1083 ♥ AQ1094 ♦ KJ3 ♣ 3	1♥ ?	1♠	Bid 2♠. LIMIT. You have found a FIT. Now you must LIMIT your hand as a MINI opener.
2. ♠ K108 ♥ AQ1042 ♦ AK2 ♣ 93	1♥ ?	2♥	Bid 3♥. LIMIT to INVITE. You have found a FIT and now you must show your MEDIUM hand and INVITE GAME.
3. ♠ KQ8 ♥ AQJ103 ♦ AK2 ♣ 93	1♥ ?	2♥	Bid 4♥. You have a MAXI hand and partner has a MINI. MINI + MAXI = GAME
4. ♠ Q82 ♥ AQJ103 ♦ AK2 ♣ K9	1♥ ?	1♠	JUMP TO 2 NT. Partner has NOT LIMITED his hand. You must LIMIT yours to show your MAXI opener. You don't have a FIT so you jump in NO TRUMP. (If you had four spades you would jump to game in spades.)
5. ♠ K1083 ♥ AQ10 ♦ KJ32 ♣ 32	1♦ ?	1♥	Bid 1♠. You could LIMIT your hand by bidding 1 NT BUT you want to EXPLORE first and see if you have a spade fit.
6. ♠ K108 ♥ AQ10 ♦ KJ32 ♣ 1032	1♦ ?	1♥	Bid 1 NT. LIMIT. Now responder knows what HAND COMBO you have.
7. ♠ AK103 ♥ AQJ ♦ AJ102 ♣ 102	1♦ 1♠ ?	1♥ 3♠	Bid 5♠. INVITING SLAM. Partner has shown a MEDIUM hand by raising your spades two levels. You have a MAXI hand. MAXI + MEDIUM = INVITE SLAM.
8. ♠ AKQ3 ♥ AQJ102 ♦ A10 ♣ 32	1♥ ?	3♥	Bid 5♥. INVITING SLAM. Partner has shown a MEDIUM hand and you have a MAXI hand.
9. ♠ AKQ3 ♥ AQJ102 ♦ A103 ♣ 2	1♥ ?	4♥	Bid 6♥. Responder has shown a MAXI hand and you have a MAXI. MAXI + MAXI = SLAM.

Review

YOUR HAND:	YOU BID	PARTNER BIDS	ANSWER
10. ♠ J104 ♡ AQJ932 ◇ AQ ♣ 102	1♡ ?	1♠	REBID 2♡. You don't have a SPADE fit and you want to LIMIT your hand. You have six hearts so you can bid them again.
11. ♠ A104 ♡ AQJ932 ◇ AQ ♣ 102	1♡ ?	1♠	REBID 3♡. You can JUMP REBID your suit to show six or more and a MEDIUM hand.
12. ♠ A1042 ♡ AQ9 ◇ J102 ♣ K98	1♣ 1♠ ?	1♡ 2♣	PASS. Responder has shown a MINI hand and you have a MINI hand. MINI + MINI = NO chance for game.
13. ♠ A1042 ♡ AQ9 ◇ J1092 ♣ K9	1◇ 1♠ ?	1♡ 1NT	PASS. Responder is showing a MINI hand, this time with no fit for you.
14. ♠ A1042 ♡ AQ9 ◇ J1092 ♣ K9	1◇ 1♠ ?	1♡ 2◇	PASS. Again, partner has shown a MINI hand.
15. ♠ QJ ♡ A1093 ◇ KQ1094 ♣ Q2	1◇ ?	1♠	Here you have a choice! You could bid 1 NT or 2◇. Both bids would show your MINI hand.
16. ♠ QJ ♡ A10932 ◇ KQ109 ♣ Q2	1♡ ?	2♣	REBID 2◇. Partner's bid is FORCING for one round.

COMPETITION

the bidding wars

In every hand there is an OPENER.
and then there is a RESPONDER.
BUT that's only TWO people!

There are **4** people at the table. Just because the other two people aren't OPENER and RESPONDER doesn't mean they won't be bidding! If your OPPONENTS are the OPENER and RESPONDER, you and PARTNER are still allowed to bid! You can't OPEN when someone has already opened. **BUT** you can OVERCALL.

overcalls

An OVERCALL is a bid made after one team has already OPENED the bidding.

If the person to your right makes an OPENING BID and you now bid a suit, you are making an OVERCALL. If the person to your left makes an OPENING BID and your partner bids a suit, that is an OVERCALL.

ANYTIME YOU BID AFTER THE OPPONENTS HAVE OPENED OR RESPONDED, YOU ARE MAKING AN OVERCALL.

OR YOU ARE ANSWERING PARTNER'S OVERCALL.

When all of this starts to happen, you are taking part in what we may call a BIDDING WAR. You and your opponents are now in a friendly fight TO WIN THE FINAL CONTRACT.

WHAT YOU NEED TO MAKE AN overcall

- ➧ 5 CARDS (OR MORE) IN THE SUIT YOU BID!

- ➧ 8 HCP (OR MORE) IF YOUR OVERCALL IS ON THE ONE-LEVEL.

- ➧ 10 HCP (OR MORE) IF YOUR OVERCALL IS ON THE TWO-LEVEL.

- ➧ 13 HCP (OR MORE) IF YOUR OVERCALL IS ON THE THREE-LEVEL OR HIGHER.

- ➧ 15-17 HCP AND A BALANCED HAND IF YOUR OVERCALL IS **1NT**.

☆ You don't NEED to wait for opening points before you can make an OVERCALL. Just be sure you have 5 or more cards in your suit.

☆ If your OVERCALL BID is **NT**, though, you need the same kind of hand as you would need to open **1NT**. Also, it's a good idea to have some good cards in the opponent's bid suit which you are overcalling.

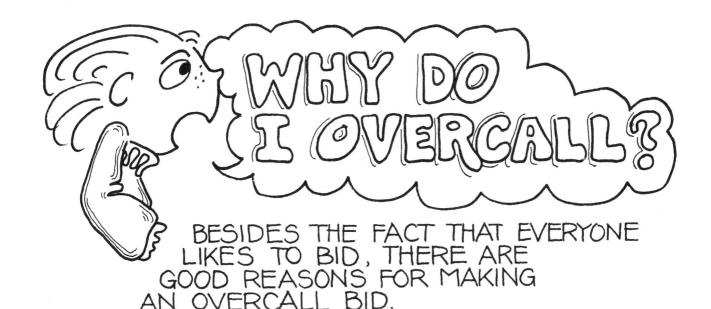

WHY DO I OVERCALL?

BESIDES THE FACT THAT EVERYONE LIKES TO BID, THERE ARE GOOD REASONS FOR MAKING AN OVERCALL BID.

① TO TELL PARTNER WHAT SUIT TO LEAD.

If the opponents win the CONTRACT, partner might have to be the opening leader. It might help him if he knew he could lead your suit!

➤OF COURSE, you are sort of promising that you will win a trick or two if he leads your suit.
SO, you really should have
some HONOR CARDS
in the suit that you OVERCALLED.

② TO TELL PARTNER THAT YOU HAVE SOME POINTS AND A LONG SUIT.

If partner also has
some points AND a FIT,
then your might WIN the CONTRACT.
Partner might even
bid a NEW SUIT to see
If you have a fit with his suit.

③ TO MAKE IT HARD FOR THE OPPONENTS TO KNOW WHETHER THEY SHOULD BID A PARTIAL, A GAME, OR A SLAM.

It would be nice if OPENER and RESPONDER could keep the bidding all to themselves. When the other people start bidding, too, it gets harder and harder for OPENER and RESPONDER to describe their hands to one another.

DOUBLE!

Let's pretend that you are playing BRIDGE right now. Your opponents have bid their way up to a CONTRACT. Because of your high card points and maybe the number of trumps which you hold, you don't think that they will win all the tricks they need. You are so happy because you know that they are going to GO DOWN and your team is going to get a PLUS SCORE.

There is a way to get an even BIGGER PLUS SCORE! You can say DOUBLE when it is your turn to bid.

To say DOUBLE to a CONTRACT means that if the CONTRACT GOES DOWN, you and partner will get about DOUBLE the PLUS SCORE.

BUT

If the OPPONENTS make the tricks they need, (or even more), the OPPONENTS will get about DOUBLE their PLUS SCORE.

It is exciting to DOUBLE a CONTRACT, but be quite sure it is GOING DOWN! Otherwise the other team could win a LOT of EXTRA SCORING POINTS!

⟹ OF COURSE, YOU DON'T EVER DOUBLE YOUR PARTNER!

One of the rules of playing bridge is that you are only allowed to DOUBLE the bid of either of your OPPONENTS. As long as the last bid was made by the opponents, and NOT by partner, you can DOUBLE.

These DOUBLES are called: PENALTY DOUBLES

TAKE-OUT DOUBLES

DOUBLES

OVER [1] MILLION SERVED

There is one kind of DOUBLE that we don't use as a PENALTY DOUBLE.
Any double of an OPPONENT'S bid on the

ONE-LEVEL by you or partner

is NOT A PENALTY DOUBLE.

It is called a **TAKE-OUT DOUBLE**.
Take-out Doubles tell partner something. They say, "Partner, I have at least 10 HCP and 3 or more cards in every suit EXCEPT the one the opponents have bid." TAKE-OUT DOUBLES come in handy when you have no 5-card or longer suit to overcall. You have points, but nothing to bid. SO - you DOUBLE and tell partner that whatever his suit is, you have a FIT for that suit. You are saying you have no more than 2 cards in the OPPONENT'S SUIT.

LOOK

IF YOU DOUBLE:

1♣ ⟶ You are saying you have ◇s, ♡s, and ♠s.
1◇ ⟶ You are showing ♣s, ♡s, and ♠s.
1♡ ⟶ You are saying you have ♣s, ◇s, and ♠s.
1♠ ⟶ You are showing ♣s, ◇s, and ♡s.

☆ When you make a take-out double, you want partner to bid, so this is basically FORCING. Partner may pass if the opponent to your left makes a bid.
☆ Partner RESPONDS his best suit with 0-9 HCP.
   Partner JUMP RESPONDS his best suit with 10+ HCP.

Review overcalls and TAKE-OUT DOUBLES

In each of the hands below your RIGHT HAND OPPONENT has OPENED 1♣.

What is your Bid?

YOUR HAND IS: YOUR BID IS:

1. ♠ J75
   ♡ KQ842
   ◇ AQ10
   ♣ 98

2. ♠ Q1098
   ♡ KQ64
   ◇ AQ9
   ♣ 64

3. ♠ A84
   ♡ AQ7
   ◇ A109
   ♣ Q432

4. ♠ 106
   ♡ KQ1074
   ◇ A10982
   ♣ 5

5. ♠ A10983
   ♡ KQ972
   ◇ 108
   ♣ 3

6. ♠ 109863
   ♡ A42
   ◇ J10
   ♣ J103

YOUR HAND IS: YOUR BID IS:

7. ♠ QJ10
   ♡ AK9863
   ◇ KJ3
   ♣ 8

8. ♠ QJ10
   ♡ AK986
   ◇ 10932
   ♣ 8

9. ♠ AK953
   ♡ 1032
   ◇ 10932
   ♣ J

10. ♠ QJ10
    ♡ AK98
    ◇ 109832
    ♣ 8

part five

USING THIS BOOK

A Basic Guide for Teachers, Parents and Bridge Players

Learning to play bridge is an easy process for children who love to play cards. With this book, we have tried to make their introduction to the game as logical, as simple and as much FUN as possible.

The book is laid out in the 'activity-book' form familiar to children. Also included are fun pages, puzzles and projects. The emphasis is on the recreational nature of the game. It is of utmost importance that the early learning experience be enjoyable.

The basic teaching technique should be to have learners doing each section of the book up to a review. The review pages will test what has been assimilated. If necessary, the section can be re-done. Typically, those learning will gradually build up a general picture of how the game is played. The book has been broken down in such a way as to ease this integrative process.

It is a good idea to have the kids begin to PLAY as soon as they have learned enough to sit at the table. They can begin with WHIST as taught in Part One. Playing Whist will familiarize the students with dealing and handling cards, rotation of play, and the practice of winning tricks as well as playing with a trump suit. One of the keys to learning is REPETITION. The more often a child uses a bit of knowledge, the better chance of that 'bit' being retained. The idea of a BRIDGE CLUB satisfies the needs of the student in two ways: 1) it provides enough players to play a game — children from smaller families may have difficulty in finding three other people to play with! 2) it provides the student with lots of opportunity to sit at the table — the bottom line to learning bridge is 'time at the table.' And, as you probably already know as a parent, kids love clubs! An industrious teacher might even pre-arrange hands to fit specific lessons .

We recommend that you, as instructor or resource person, read through this book. A good understanding of our methods and system will be valuable when helping the student(s).

The bidding system used in this book is basic Standard American. Those of you familiar with duplicate bridge will recognize the five-card major style, intermediate 1 NT openings (15-17), constructive limit bids and strong two's. Those of you who play home bridge only need not be dismayed with seemingly 'advanced' bidding techniques. There is only one 'convention' (Stayman) and if you read the book through you will find the contents quite familiar.

This first book covers only the basic mechanics of play and teaches only the preliminaries of hand evaluation. We cover high card points and fit-finding only. Then we proceed with an extensive coverage of bidding basics.

The reasons for this are three-fold.

First, we believe that a solid foundation in bidding is essential to become skillful at the game. Good bidding promotes partnership harmony!

Secondly, we feel that using 'Goren' points (extra points for shape) is best introduced after the new player has grasped the fundamentals of card play, the value of a fit and why short suits and voids can be valuable. We have emphasized the DECK as 40 points and have encouraged the student to be constantly aware of how much of the deck she and partner have between them. We believe that this approach will encourage LOGICAL thinking at the table rather than memorization.

Thirdly, the play of the hand is instruction on its own. New players will learn about finesses, card establishment, and so on, as they go. In the sequel to this first book, we will consolidate this process.

EXPLANATION OF SCORING

Although scoring is an important part of bridge, children are often bogged down by the mechanics of all the calculations involved. What we have done is presented them a SCORING CHART in the back of this book. This chart shows all the scores for all the possible contracts. It also shows scores for doubled contracts. What the chart doesn't mention is VULNERABLE scores. This is because we have not taught the reader about vulnerability in this first book.

If you are a rubber player, this scoring chart may seem a bit strange. It is the method of scoring used in 'Chicago' and duplicate bridge. The main difference is the adding of a BONUS score for all games and slams.

There is also a section on RUBBER SCORING. If your child or children are interested in 'how to score' they can learn from these pages, perhaps with a bit of your help. We strongly suggest, however, that rubber bridge scoring be encouraged only with those students genuinely interested.

The world of bridge is a varied and exciting place. This book gives a view of it from the basic unit of four players all the way up to tournaments involving thousands from many countries. The new player should be made aware of the many opportunities there are in the world of bridge — from home bridge, through local clubs, right up to international events.

ONE OF THE MORE IMPORTANT ASPECTS OF THE BOOK IS THE EMPHASIS ON PARTNER-SHIP AND TEAMWORK, ON SPORTSMANSHIP AND FAIR PLAY, ON POLITENESS AND COURTESY. THESE QUALITIES SHOULD BE NURTURED ABOVE ALL THE OTHERS.

Inquiries about this book and the sequel may be made to:

Andrew Bernstein
Pando Publications
Department KB
540 Longleaf Drive
Roswell, Georgia 30075

Best of luck in the world of bridge!

SCORING

HERE IS AN EASY-TO-USE CHART FOR SCORING.
THIS CHART WILL SHOW YOU ALL THE BIDS
OR CONTRACTS AND ALL THE SCORES YOU GET.
* IF YOU GO DOWN IN YOUR CONTRACT, SEE PAGE **176** FOR THE POINTS YOU LOSE.

IF YOU BID	AND YOU WIN BOOK (6 TRICKS) PLUS THIS MANY MORE TRICKS	YOU WILL SCORE	OR, IF YOU WERE DOUBLED YOU WILL SCORE
1♣ or 1♦	1	70	140
	2	90	240
	3	110	340
	4	130	440
	5	150	540
	6	170	640
	7	190	740
1♡ or 1♠	1	80	160
	2	110	260
	3	140	360
	4	170	460
	5	200	560
	6	230	660
	7	260	760
1 No Trump	1	90	180
	2	120	280
	3	150	380
	4	180	480
	5	210	580
	6	240	680
	7	270	780
2♣ or 2♦	2	90	180
	3	110	280
	4	130	380
	5	150	480
	6	170	580
	7	190	680
2♡ or 2♠	2	110	470
	3	140	570
	4	170	670
	5	200	770
	6	230	870
	7	260	970
2 No Trump	2	120	490
	3	150	590
	4	180	690
	5	210	790
	6	240	890
	7	270	990

IF YOU BID	AND YOU WIN BOOK (6 TRICKS) PLUS THIS MANY MORE TRICKS	YOU WILL SCORE	OR, IF YOU WERE DOUBLED YOU WILL SCORE
3♣ or 3♦	3	110	470
	4	130	570
	5	150	670
	6	170	770
	7	190	870
3♡ or 3♠	3	140	530
	4	170	630
	5	200	730
	6	230	830
	7	260	930
3 No Trump	3	400	550
	4	430	650
	5	460	750
	6	490	850
	7	520	950
4♣ or 4♦	4	130	510
	5	150	610
	6	170	710
	7	190	810
4♡ or 4♠	4	420	590
	5	450	690
	6	480	790
	7	510	890
4 No Trump	4	430	610
	5	460	710
	6	490	810
	7	520	910
5♣ or 5♦	5	400	550
	6	420	650
	7	440	750
5♡ or 5♠	5	450	650
	6	480	750
	7	510	850
5 No Trump	5	460	670
	6	490	770
	7	520	870
6♣ or 6♦	6	920	1090
	7	940	1190
6♡ or 6♠	6	980	1210
	7	1010	1310
6 No Trump	6	990	1230
	7	1020	1330
7♣ or 7♦	7	1440	1630
7♡ ot 7♠	7	1510	1770
7 No Trump	7	1520	1790

ADVANCED SCORING
rubber bridge

Many bridge players use
a kind of scoring called   RUBBER BRIDGE
SCORING. This is a fun way to score at bridge.
If you are an eager learner you might want to learn
how to do it.
In RUBBER SCORING, each trick you bid and win
scores a certain number of points. If this adds up to
100, you have a game. If you score 2 GAMES, you win
the rubber. A RUBBER is the best 2 out of 3 games,
just as in many other sports and games.
The scoresheet is drawn as you learned before, but
with a line across the middle:

WE	THEY
BONUS and OVERTRICKS	BONUS and OVERTRICKS
GAME 100 OR MORE SCORING POINTS	
	GAME

ABOVE THE LINE

BELOW THE LINE

The points you get for
bidding and winning tricks
are scored BELOW THE LINE.
If you win more tricks than
what you bid, the extra
points are scored
ABOVE THE LINE.
If you GO DOWN, those
points score for the other
team ABOVE THE LINE.
If your score BELOW THE LINE
adds up to 100 or more, then
you have a GAME, and you
draw an arrow to show it,
pointing to your side. And
the same for your opponents.

The first team to get 2 games out of 3 wins the rubber and
gets a BONUS SCORE ABOVE THE LINE. If a team wins 2 games
before the other team wins 1, this is called a FAST RUBBER,
and scores a bonus of 700 ABOVE THE LINE. If a team wins
2 games, while the other team is winning 1, this is called
a SLOW RUBBER – the bonus is 500 points ABOVE THE LINE.
The only points scored below the line are those earned by
bidding and making a certain number of tricks.

ADVANCED SCORING
rubber bridge
CONTINUED

You don't have to score 100 points all at once. You can add up to 100 by bidding and making PARTIALS. Of course, you must bid and make all of these partials before the opponents score a GAME. Naturally, if you and partner have enough High Card Points, you'll want to bid game.

Here is the point scoring for RUBBER BRIDGE.

RUBBER SCORING SHEET

IF YOU BID AND MAKE A CERTAIN NUMBER OF TRICKS IN :	YOU SCORE :
♣s or ♢s	20 points for each trick bid and made, scored BELOW THE LINE. 20 points for each overtrick, scored ABOVE THE LINE.
♡s or ♤s	30 points for each trick bid and made, scored BELOW THE LINE. 30 points for each overtrick scored ABOVE THE LINE.
NT (NO TRUMP)	40 points for the 1st trick, 30 points for each other trick, scored BELOW THE LINE. 30 points for each overtrick scored ABOVE THE LINE
BONUS SCORES	fast rubber 700 points slow rubber 500 points each ABOVE THE LINE.

VULNERABLE If your side has one game made, and you are still playing to win the rubber, you are VULNERABLE. If you go down you will lose more points than when you were NOT VULNERABLE. You will want to be more careful.

VULNERABLE (CONTINUED)

The GOOD thing about being VULNERABLE is that,
if you are doubled and make overtricks, you get extra
points for each one.
Another good thing about being VULNERABLE - you
get an extra bonus for a small slam, or a grand slam.

SLAM BONUSES These are BIG bonuses!

Small slam, not vulnerable	500 points	ABOVE THE LINE
Small slam, vulnerable	750 points	ABOVE THE LINE
Grand slam, not vulnerable	1000 points	ABOVE THE LINE
Grand slam, vulnerable	1500 points	ABOVE THE LINE

DOUBLED SCORES How to score when you are DOUBLED.

DID YOU MAKE YOUR CONTRACT?
  If yes;
    1. double your score below the line, if this is more
       than 100 points - that's a GAME!
    2. add a bonus of 50 points above the line.
    3. give yourself 100 points for each overtrick
         if you were NOT VULNERABLE
    OR give yourself 200 points for each overtrick
       if you were VULNERABLE.
       These points are scored ABOVE THE LINE.
  If no;
How to score if you didn't make your contract.
Your opponents score this many points ABOVE THE LINE:

YOU WENT DOWN	NOT VULNERABLE NOT DOUBLED	NOT VULNERABLE DOUBLED	VULNERABLE NOT DOUBLED	VULNERABLE DOUBLED
ONE TRICK	50	100	100	200
TWO TRICKS	100	300	200	500
THREE TRICKS	150	500	300	800
FOUR TRICKS	200	700	400	1100
FIVE TRICKS	250	900	500	1400
SIX TRICKS	300	1100	600	1700
SEVEN TRICKS	350	1300	700	2000

We hope that you never go down more than seven tricks!

LET'S GET TO KNOW EACH OTHER!

IN THE WORLD OF BRIDGE THERE ARE MANY FRIENDS JUST WAITING TO BE INTRODUCED.

WRITE!

We would love to hear from you! Write to us and tell us how you liked our book. We'd like to hear about you learning to play bridge. And we would love to hear any funny stories, too.

PEN PALS

Would you like to exchange letters with other kids who are learning to play bridge? (Or who already know how?). If you do, we'll help. When you write to us, print your name and address clearly at the bottom of your letter, with 'PEN PAL' printed next to it; we'll send you a list of addresses of other kids.

WRITE TO US: JUDE GOODWIN and DON ELLISON
BOX 339
ROSSLAND, B.C.
CANADA, V0G 1Y0

ANSWER PAGES

WHAT DO YOU KNOW?   Page 14

1. 52
2. ♣ (clubs) ♢ (diamonds)
   ♡ (hearts) ♠ (spades)
3. 13
4. AKQJ1098765432
5. AKQJ
6. 1098765432
7. Nine
8. One
9. Four

10. Four
11. 13
12. ♠ ♡ ♢ ♣
13. ♠
14. ♣
15. ♣ and ♢
16. ♡ and ♠
17. ♡
18. ♡

19. ♢
20. a) A   d) 7
    b) 9   e) A
    c) K   f) A
21. a) ♠
    b) ♡
    c) ♠
    d) ♠

FUN PAGE   Page 25

KOKANEE BRIDGE CLUB

Monday	Tuesday	Wednesday	Thursday	Friday	Saturday
Betty	Pat	Betty	John	Betty	John
Pat	Lori	John	Lori	Pat	Lori
				John	
				Lori	

ODD PICTURE: 2 doesn't belong because it is the thing without legs!
TIME PUZZLE: Three hours
HOW MANY KIDS!?: Three

TEST YOURSELF   Page 34

1. S   2. W   3. S   4. W   5. E   6. N

COUNT YOUR HAND   Page 38

1.	5	2.	7	3.	2	4.	7	5.	0	6.	10
	2		7		0		3		5		2
	4		2		7		0		0		7
	4		0		1		7		1		1
	15		16		10		17		6		20

7. 40   8. 10   9. a) 4 b) 3 c) 2 d) 1 e) 3 f) 6 g) 7 h) 5 i) 5   10. #6   11. #5

LOOK AT THE LADDER   Page 41

1. 3 NT   4♣   4♢   4♡   4♠   4 NT   5♣
2. 2♠   2 NT   3♣   3♢   3♡   3♠   3 NT
3. 1♡   1♠   1 NT   2♣   2♢   2♡   2♠   2 NT
4. 4♡   4♠   4 NT   5♣   5♢   5♡   5♠   5 NT   6♣   6♢   6♡
5. 5♣   5♢   5♡   5♠   5 NT   6♣   6♢
6. 1 NT   2♣   2♢   2♡   2♠   2 NT   3♣   3♢   3♡   3♠   3 NT
7. There are five one-bids. They are 1♣   1♢   1♡   1♠   1 NT.
8. There are five three-bids. They are 3♣   3♢   3♡   3♠   3 NT.

HERE ARE ALL THE BIDS   Page 42

7 NT   6 tricks + 7 more (13 tricks) if nothing is trump
7♠   6 tricks + 7 more (13 tricks) if ♠ is trump
7♡   6 tricks + 7 more (13 tricks) if ♡ is trump
7♢   6 tricks + 7 more (13 tricks) if ♢ is trump
7♣   6 tricks + 7 more (13 tricks) if ♣ is trump
6 NT   6 tricks + 6 more (12 tricks) if nothing is trump
6♠   6 tricks + 6 more (12 tricks) if ♠ is trump
6♡   6 tricks + 6 more (12 tricks) if ♡ is trump
6♢   6 tricks + 6 more (12 tricks) if ♢ is trump
6♣   6 tricks + 6 more (12 tricks) if ♣ is trump
5 NT   6 tricks + 5 more (11 tricks) if nothing is trump
5♠   6 tricks + 5 more (11 tricks) if ♠ is trump
5♡   6 tricks + 5 more (11 tricks) if ♡ is trump
5♢   6 tricks + 5 more (11 tricks) if ♢ is trump
5♣   6 tricks + 5 more (11 tricks) if ♣ is trump
4 NT   6 tricks + 4 more (10 tricks) if nothing is trump
5♠   6 tricks + 4 more (10 tricks) if ♠ is trump
4♡   6 tricks + 4 more (10 tricks) if ♡ is trump
4♢   6 tricks + 4 more (10 tricks) if ♢ is trump
4♣   6 tricks + 4 more (10 tricks) if ♣ is trump
3 NT   6 tricks + 3 more (9 tricks) if nothing is trump
3♠   6 tricks + 3 more (9 tricks) if ♠ is trump
3♡   6 tricks + 3 more (9 tricks) if ♡ is trump
3♢   6 tricks + 3 more (9 tricks) if ♢ is trump
3♣   6 tricks + 3 more (9 tricks) if ♣ is trump
2 NT   6 tricks + 2 more (8 tricks) if nothing is trump
2♠   6 tricks + 2 more (8 tricks) if ♠ is trump
2♡   6 tricks + 2 more (8 tricks) if ♡ is trump
2♢   6 tricks + 2 more (8 tricks) if ♢ is trump
2♣   6 tricks + 2 more (8 tricks) if ♣ is trump
1 NT   6 tricks + 1 more (7 tricks) if nothing is trump
1♠   6 tricks + 1 more (7 tricks) if ♠ is trump
1♡   6 tricks + 1 more (7 tricks) if ♡ is trump
1♢   6 tricks + 1 more (7 tricks) if ♢ is trump
1♣   6 tricks + 1 more (7 tricks) if ♣ is trump

WHAT DO YOU KNOW?   Page 43

1.   The BOOK is the first six tricks.
2.   a)   4 NT   6 tricks + 4 more with nothing as trump
      b)   2♠   6 tricks + 2 more with ♠ as trump
      c)   1 NT   6 tricks + 1 more with nothing as trump
      d)   3♣   6 tricks + 3 more with ♣ as trump
      e)   2♢   6 tricks + 2 more with ♢ as trump
      f)   3♡   6 tricks + 3 more with ♡ as trump
      g)   5♠   6 tricks + 5 more with ♠ as trump
      h)   4♢   6 tricks + 4 more with ♢ as trump
      i)   6♡   6 tricks + 6 more with ♡ as trump
      j)   3♢   6 tricks + 3 more with ♢ as trump
      k)   2 NT   6 tricks + 2 more with nothing as trump
      l)   7♡   6 tricks + 7 more with ♡ as trump

m) 5♣ 6 tricks + 5 more with ♣ as trump
n) 3 NT 6 tricks + 3 more with nothing as trump
o) 4♡ 6 tricks + 4 more with ♡ as trump
p) 2◇ 6 tricks + 2 more with ◇ as trump
q) 1 NT 6 tricks + 1 more with nothing as trump
r) 3♠ 6 tricks + 3 more with ♠ as trump
s) 5 NT 6 tricks + 5 more with nothing as trump
t) 6♡ 6 tricks + 6 more with ♡ as trump

3. a) 9 b) 10 c) 11 d) 12 e) 7 f) 8 g) 11 h) 10
4. a) You can lose four tricks.   c) You can lose two tricks.
   b) You can lose three tricks. d) You can't lose ANY tricks.

THINK ABOUT IT   Page 48

If you are in the following contracts how many tricks can you lose?

1 NT—Six
3♡—Four
7♠—None
4♣—Three
5◇—Two
2♡—Five
6♣—One
4♡—Three
1♠—Six

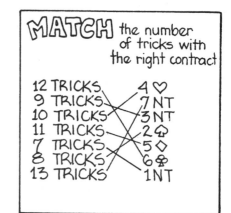

IAN'S TRICKS

Ian's opponents won seven tricks.
Ian's opponents lost six tricks.
Ian won six tricks.
Ian's opponents did NOT make their contract
   —they needed to win eight tricks to
   make 2 NT.

WHAT DO YOU KNOW?   Page 50
1. The last bid made before three passes is the final CONTRACT.
2. NT CONTRACTS score the most points.
3. MINOR SUIT CONTRACTS score the least points.
4. GAME CONTRACTS are SPECIAL because you get BONUS POINTS if you bid them.
5. GAME in NT is 3 NT.
6. You need nine tricks to make GAME in NT.
7. You need 10 tricks to make GAME in the MAJOR SUITS.
8. You need 11 tricks to make GAME in the MINOR SUITS.
9. GAMES in the MAJOR SUITS are 4♠ and 4♡.
10. GAMES in the MINOR SUITS are 5♣ and 5◇.
11. You don't get your GAME BONUS SCORE unless YOU BID TO THE GAME.
12. 4♡   4♠   5♣   5◇   3 NT
13. a) 5◇   b) 4♠   c) 2♡   d) 5♣   e) 6◇   f) They both need the same.

FUN PAGE   Page 57
SAME CARDS: Amber's hand

WHO WON?   Page 57
1. W
2. S
3. E
4. N
5. S
6. E
7. E
8. E

FIND 'A' WORD

```
C L U B S R E D N A M O
S R E Z T I B I K A A A
D Z W I N R M P N R N W
I S P B H L I D P B D H
A P M R V E Z C M T E P
M A I I S A A K U U R A
O R R D P D N R R B U U
N T B G I M F A T Z I S
D R Z E K A T N E S L H
S U I T K H M K D B T E
R E N T R A P O S I S L
W H I S T R U P A K B L
W L S L N M A N C D P O
K H C A R D S A L A T
R W I N E D R S V R U
B R I D G T S M I L E B
```

WHAT DO YOU KNOW?   Page 63
1. 13
2. You need eight cards for a fit.
3. You want to have at least three more trumps than the opponents.
4. The four different kinds of fit are: 4-4   5-3   6-2   7-1.
5. The best kind of fit is where the cards are divided evenly between your hand and partner's hand.
6. a) Best fit: ♠
   Kind of fit: 5-3
   b) Best fit: ♡
   Kind of fit: 6-2
   c) Best fit: ♡
   Kind of fit: 4-4
   d) Best fit: ♡
   Kind of fit: 5-3
   e) Best fit: ♣
   Kind of fit: 5-4

THE BIDDING MAZE   Page 64

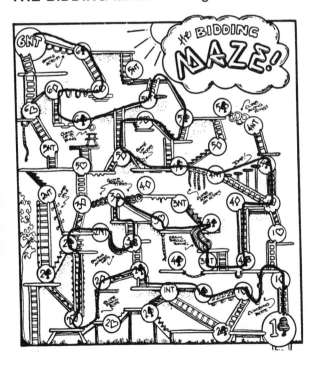

TEST YOURSELF   Page 65
1. For FUN
2. 52
3. Four
4. AKQJ1098765432
5. ♠ ♡ ◊ ♣
6. AKQJ
7. Ace
8. Two
9. ♠ ♡ ◊ ♣
10. ♠ and ♡
11. ♣ and ◊
12. Four
13. Four
14. One
15. To the left
16. 13
17. A trick is one card from each player gathered into a group.

18. A trick is won by the player who played the highest ranking card or the highest trump card.
19. The leader in whist is the person to the left of the dealer.
20. The leader in bridge is the person to the left of the person who won the contract.
21. A hand is what you call the cards you are dealt.
22. Wild cards in whist and bridge are called TRUMPS.
23. The RULE about PLAYING TO A TRICK: You must follow suit!
24. You can play a trump card when you have no cards in the suit led.
25. A trump will lose a trick when a higher trump is played.
26. Yes, you are allowed to lead a trump.
27. A GOOD HAND has lots of honor cards.
28. If you play whist with a partner you need FOUR players.
29. YOUR PARTNER is on your team.
30. THE OPPONENTS are the people on each side of you.
31. Your partner sits across the table from you.
32. Each person gets 13 cards when there are four players (13 + 13 + 13 + 13 = 52).
33. 13 tricks can be won.
34. KIBITZERS are what we call people who are watching a game of bridge.
35. The four parts of bridge are: The deal, the bidding, the play and the scoring.
36.   37.

38. A = 4 HCP   K = 3 HCP   Q = 2 HCP   J = 1 HCP
39. There are 10 HCP in one suit. There are 40 HCP in the deck.
40. a) 10 HCP   d) 3 HCP
    b) 12 HCP   e) 12 HCP
    c) 23 HCP   f) 5 HCP
41. The BOOK is the first six tricks.
42. a) 7 tricks   h) 7 tricks
    b) 8 tricks   i) 9 tricks
    c) 9 tricks   j) 13 tricks
    d) 9 tricks   k) 8 tricks
    e) 10 tricks   l) 11 tricks
    f) 12 tricks   m) 10 tricks
    g) 13 tricks   n) 9 tricks
43. 1♣ 1♦ 1♡ 1♠ 1NT
44. 6♣ 6♦ 6♡ 6♠ 6 NT
45. There are seven bidding levels.
46. Say PASS when you don't want to bid.
47. The bidding is over when there are three passes in a row.
48. The main rule about bidding is that each bid must be higher than the last bid.
49. The bidding goes around to the left.
50. The dealer starts the bidding.
51. There are 35 bids altogether, 5 for each level.
52. There are five bids on each level.
53. THE CONTRACT is the last bid made before three passes.
54. The contract tells us what is trump and how many tricks declarer has to win.
55. MINOR SUIT CONTRACTS score the fewest points.
56. GAME CONTRACTS are special because they earn you a BONUS SCORE.

57. a) 5♣   c) 4♡   e) 3 NT
    b) 5♢   d) 4♠

58. a) A MINOR SUIT GAME requires 11 TRICKS.
    b) A MAJOR SUIT GAME requires 10 TRICKS.
    c) A NT GAME requires 9 TRICKS.

59. Minor suits are unpopular because their contracts score the fewest points and their games need the most number of tricks.

60. THE RULE ABOUT GAME CONTRACTS is that GAME CONTRACTS MUST BE BID TO EARN THE BONUS SCORE.

61. 6♣ 6♢ 6♡ 6♠ 6 NT

62. 7♣ 7♢ 7♡ 7♠ 7 NT

63. You need to take 12 TRICKS to make a SMALL SLAM. You need to take 13 TRICKS to make a GRAND SLAM.

64. You can lose ONE TRICK and still make a SMALL SLAM. You can lose NO TRICKS and still make a GRAND SLAM.

65. When a contract is won by a team, THE DECLARER is the person who BID THE TRUMP SUIT FIRST, or, if the contract is in NT, the person who bid NT first.

66. DUMMY is DECLARER'S PARTNER.

67. The person TO THE LEFT OF DECLARER MAKES THE OPENING LEAD.

68. Dummy's cards go down on the table after the opening lead.

69. DECLARER plays the cards from the dummy.

70. THE DEFENDERS are the opponents of declarer and dummy.

71. The defenders are trying to win enough tricks so that declarer doesn't make his contract.

72. GOING DOWN means that you didn't take enough tricks to make your contract.

73. MAKING YOUR CONTRACT means that you won at least the number of tricks promised by your contract.

74. Two reasons for bidding are:
    1. To pick a trump suit or to decide to play in NT.
    2. To find out how high to bid.

75. A FIT is eight or more cards in one suit between your hand and partner's hand.

76. You need a fit so your team will have more trumps than the opponents.

77. 4-4   5-3   6-2   7-1

WHAT DO YOU KNOW?   Page 72

1. How many HCP? 15   Is it an opening hand? Yes
   What kind of opening hand? MEDIUM
2. How many HCP? 10   Is it an opening hand? No
3. How many HCP? 13   Is it an opening hand? Yes
   What kind of opening hand? MINI
4. How many HCP? 20   Is an an opening hand? Yes
   What kind of opening hand? MAXI
5. How many HCP? 4   Is it an opening hand? No
6. How many HCP? 13   Is it an opening hand? Yes
   What kind of opening hand? MINI
7. You need 13 or more High Card Points to open.

WHAT IS YOUR OPENING BID?   Page 74
1. 1♠   4. 1♢   7. 1♣   10. 1♣
2. 1♡   5. 1♡   8. 1♠
3. 1♢   6. 1♢   9. 1♢

WHAT IS YOUR OPENING BID?   Page 76

1. 1 NT
2. 1♠
3. 1♡—don't open 1 NT with five-card major.
4. 1 NT
5. Pass
6. 1♣—remember, you need 15-17 to open 1 NT.
7. 1 NT—you can open 1 NT with five-card minor.
8. 1♢

9. 1♡
10. 1♠
11. Pass
12. 1♣
13. 1♠
14. 1♡
15. 1 NT
16. 1♣

WHAT IS YOUR OPENING BID?   Page 78

1. 2♠
2. 2 NT
3. 6 NT
4. 1♡
5. 1♣. You plan to jump in NT to show your big hand.
6. 2NT

7. 2 NT
8. 2♡
9. 4 NT
10. 1♢
11. 1♣
12. 2♣

FUN WITH WORDS   Page 79

AK fifth AK763
QJ third QJ4
Stiff K . . . . K
Rag dub . . . . 32 (dub stands for doubleton)
KQ tight . . . . KQ
Stiff 10 10
Q dub Q8
10 9 sixth 1095432

♠ Q J 10 3   Queen jack fourth
♡ K   Stiff king
♢ AK   Ace king tight
♣ A Q J 10 9 4   Ace queen jack sixth

184

Whenever you learn something new, you learn a whole bunch of special words. Let's see if you can be a SMARTY CAT and connect each of the bridge words below with its meaning. Draw a line between them.

THE MINORS
THE BOOK
LIMIT BID
CONTRACT
THE MAJORS
GOING DOWN
GAMES
SINGLETON
RANK
LEAD
TRUMP
VOID
BALANCED HAND
PASS
RESPONDER
OPENER
HCP
ROUNDS
DOUBLETON

THE TOP TO BOTTOM ORDER OF THE CARDS AND SUITS
THE FIRST CARD PLAYED TO ANY TRICK
ONLY ONE CARD IN A SUIT
DIAMONDS AND CLUBS
WHAT YOU SAY IF YOU DON'T WANT TO BID
THE FIRST PERSON TO MAKE A BID
HIGH CARD POINTS USED TO COUNT BRIDGE HANDS
NO CARDS AT ALL IN A SUIT
SPADES AND HEARTS
A BID THAT PROMISES NO MORE THAN A CERTAIN NUMBER OF POINTS AND NO LESS THAN A CERTAIN NUMBER OF POINTS
MAKING LESS THAN THE NUMBER OF TRICKS PROMISED IN YOUR CONTRACT.
3NT, 4♡, 4♠, 5♣, 5♢
TWO CARDS IN A SUIT
THE FINAL BID - PICKING TRUMP AND PROMISING TO TAKE A CERTAIN NUMBER OF TRICKS
A HAND WITH NO SINGLETONS OR VOIDS AND NO MORE THAN ONE DOUBLETON.
A SUIT WHICH WINS A TRICK OVER ALL OTHER SUITS
THE OPENER'S PARTNER
THE FIRST SIX TRICKS
FOUR BIDS WHERE EACH PLAYER GETS ONE TURN

TEST YOURSELF   Page 87

1. 2♡   MINI responding hand with a FIT: LIMIT.
2. 4♠   MAXI responding hand with a FIT.
3. 3♠   MEDIUM responding hand with a FIT: LIMIT.
4. 3♡   MEDIUM responding hand with a FIT: LIMIT.
5. 4♡   MAXI responding hand with a FIT.
6. 2♠   MINI responding hand with a FIT.
7. The first bid made is called the OPENING BID.
8. Dealer has the first chance to make an opening bid.
9. The Opening Bidder is the first person to make a bid other than PASS.
10. The partner of the opening bidder is call the RESPONDER.
11. You need 13 or more HCP before you can open the bidding.
12. a) MINI   13-14 HCP
    b) MEDIUM   15-17 HCP
    c) MAXI   18+ HCP
13. A BALANCED HAND is a hand with no singleton or void and no more than one doubleton.
14. A SINGLETON is a suit with only one card.
15. A VOID is a suit with no cards in it.
16. You need a balanced hand, no five-card or longer major, and 15-17 HCP.
17. You need 21-24 HCP and a balanced hand.
18. a) 26 HCP   b) 28 HCP

WHAT DO YOU KNOW?   Page 91

1. I respond: 2 ♠
   My response says: I have three or more cards in partner's spade suit and 6-9 HCP.
2. I respond: 1 NT
   My response says: I have no fit for partner's suit, I don't have four spades but I do have 6-9 HCP.
3. I respond: 2 ♠
   My response says: I have a fit for partner's spades and 6-9 HCP.
4. I respond: 1 ♠
   My response says: I don't have a fit for partner's hearts, but I do have a four-card spade suit
                        and want to explore for a 4-4 spade fit. I also have six or more HCP.
5. I respond: 1 NT
   My response says: I have no fit and I have no four-card or longer spade suit. I also have no
                        less than 6 HCP and no more than 9 HCP.
6. You need 10 or more HCP to respond at the two-level.
7. You want to respond 1 ♠ if you have four spades and no fit for partner's hearts because partner
   may have four spades and then you would have found a 4-4 MAJOR SUIT FIT.

WHAT IS YOUR RESPONSE?   Page 95
PARTNER OPENS 1 ♡

1. 2 ◇   EXPLORE. Show your long suit and 10+ HCP.
2. 3 ♡   RAISE PARTNER'S HEARTS to the three-level to show your FIT and 10-12 HCP.
          (MEDIUM RESPONDING HAND)
3. 1 ♠   EXPLORE. Bid your four-card spade suit and see if partner has a fit!
4. 4 ♡   RAISE PARTNER'S HEARTS TO GAME to show your fit and your MAXI responding hand.
5. 1 ♠   EXPLORE to find your 4-4 major suit fit.
6. 2 ♣   BID FOUR-CARD SUITS UP THE LADDER when you have no fit. You have 10 or more
          points so you can bid on the two-level.
7. 2 ◇   BID YOUR LONG SUIT. You have 10 points so you can bid on the two-level.
8. 2 ♣   BID FOUR-CARD SUITS UP THE LADDER.

PARTNER OPENS 1 ♠

1. 2 ◇   BID FOUR-CARD SUITS UP THE LADDER when you have no fit and no long suit.
2. 2 ♡   BID YOUR LONG SUIT.
3. 2 ◇   BID YOUR LONG SUIT.
4. 2 ♡   BID YOUR LONG SUIT.
5. 1 NT   You can't bid four-card suits up the ladder here because you don't have enough points
          to bid on the two-level. 1 NT shows your 6-9 HCP.
6. 2 ♣   Here you can bid four-card suits UP THE LADDER.

WHAT IS YOUR RESPONSE?   Page 97
PARTNER OPENS 1 ♡

1.	4 ♡	SHOW YOUR FIT AND YOUR MAXI responding hand.
2.	1 ♠	BID FOUR-CARD SUITS UP THE LADDER.
3.	2 ♣	BID YOUR LONG SUIT.
4.	PASS	You don't have 6 HCP.
5.	2 NT	Bid 2 NT with no fit, no four-card major and a balanced hand.
6.	2 ◇	BID YOUR LONG SUIT.
7.	2 ♡	SHOW YOUR FIT and your MINI responding hand.
8.	1 ♠	BID YOUR LONG SUIT.
9.	2 ♣	BID FOUR-CARD SUITS UP THE LADDER.
10.	1 NT	You can't bid 2 ◇ because you don't have enough points to respond on the two-level. 1 NT shows your 6-9 HCP and no fit.
11.	2 ♡	SHOW YOUR FIT AND YOUR MINI responding hand.
12.	3 ♡	SHOW YOUR FIT AND YOUR MEDIUM responding hand.

WHAT IS YOUR RESPONSE?   Page 98
PARTNER OPENS 1 ♠

1.	2 ◇	BID YOUR LONG SUIT.
2.	3 ♠	RAISE PARTNER'S SUIT TO THE THREE-LEVEL to show your FIT and your MEDIUM hand.
3.	2 ♡	BID YOUR LONG SUIT.
4.	2 ◇	BID FOUR-CARD SUITS UP THE LADDER.
5.	2 ♠	SHOW YOUR FIT and your MINI responding hand.
6.	1 NT	You can't bid on the two-level because you don't have 10 or more points. 1 NT shows your MINI (6-9 HCP) responding hand and NO FIT.
7.	3 ♠	RAISE PARTNER'S SUIT to the three-level to show your FIT and your MEDIUM hand (10-12 HCP).
8.	3 ♠	SHOW YOUR FIT.
9.	3 ♠	SHOW YOUR FIT.
10.	2 ♣	BID FOUR-CARD SUITS UP THE LADDER.
11.	2 ♣	BID YOUR LONG SUIT.
12.	2 ♣	BID YOUR LONG SUIT.
13.	2 ♣	EXPLORE: BID FOUR-CARD SUITS UP THE LADDER.
14.	4 ♠	RAISE PARTNER'S SUIT to game to show your FIT and MAXI responding hand.

PARTNER OPENS 1♣

1. 1♢   BID FOUR-CARD SUITS UP THE LADDER.
2. 1♢   BID FOUR-CARD SUITS UP THE LADDER.
3. 1♡   BID FOUR-CARD SUITS UP THE LADDER.
4. 1 NT   You have a nice balanced hand, 6-9 HCP and no four-card major. Remember: you need at least five cards to support partner's minor.
5. 2♣   SHOW A FIT for partner's minor when you have five or more AND NO FOUR-CARD MAJOR.
6. 1♡   Bid a five-card suit before a four-card suit.
7. 1♡
8. 1♠
9. 1♡   BID FOUR-CARD SUITS UP THE LADDER.
10. 1 NT   SHOWING A MINI responding hand (6-9 HCP) and no four-card major.
11. 1♡   EXPLORE for a 4-4 major suit fit before showing your fit for partner's minor.
12. 2♣   SHOW A FIT for partner's minor when you have five or more and no four-card major.

PARTNER OPENS 1♣
1. 1♡   BID a four-card major before bidding NT.
2. 1♡   BID your long suit.
3. 1♢   BID FOUR-CARD SUITS UP THE LADDER.
4. 1♢   BID YOUR FOUR-CARD SUIT.
5. 3♣   Shows five or more of partner's minor and a MEDIUM responding hand.
6. 1♠   Bid a five-card suit.

PARTNER OPENS 1♢
1. 1♡   BID FOUR-CARD SUITS UP THE LADDER.
2. 2♣   You can't raise partner's diamonds because you have only four. BID YOUR LONG SUIT.
3. 2♣   Bid your four-card suit.
4. 1♡   BID FOUR-CARD SUITS UP THE LADDER.
5. 1♠   Bid your five-card or longer suit.
6. 1♠   EXPLORE for a major suit fit before showing support for partner's minor.

PARTNER OPENS 1♣
1. 1♡   EXPLORE for a 4-4 major suit fit. You can show your MAXI responding hand with your next bid.
2. 1♠   BID YOUR LONG SUIT.
3. 1♡   EXPLORE for a 4-4 major suit fit.
4. 2 NT   Show a GAME FORCE HAND with no four-card major.
5. 1♢   Plan to jump in clubs at your next turn to bid.
6. 1♢   BID FOUR-CARD SUITS UP THE LADDER.

PARTNER OPENS 1◇

1. 1♠   WITH TWO FIVE-CARD SUITS BID THE HIGHER RANKING FIRST.
2. 2♣   BID YOUR LONG SUIT.
3. 2 NT   SHOW YOUR MAXI RESPONDING HAND AND NO FOUR-CARD MAJOR by bidding 2 NT.
4. 1♡   EXPLORE for a 4-4 major suit fit.
5. 2 NT   SHOW YOUR MAXI responding hand and NO FOUR-CARD MAJOR. You could bid 2♣ here but you have no four-card major so you can describe your hand better by bidding 2 NT.
6. 1♡   EXPLORE for a 4-4 major suit.

REVIEW ALL RESPONSES TO 1♣/1◇   Page 111

1.
  a)   MINI responding hand   6-9 HCP
  b)   MEDIUM responding hand   10-12 HCP
  c)   MAXI responding hand   13 or more HCP

2.
  a)   Bid a long suit on the one-level.
  b)   Bid four-card suits up the ladder.
  c)   Bid 1 NT. A LIMIT BID showing 6-9 points and no four-card major.
  d)   Bid 2♣ with five or more.

3.
  a)   Raise partner's minor to the two-level.
  b)   Bid 1 NT.

4. You are saying you have NO FOUR-CARD MAJOR.

5.
  a)   Bid your long suit.
  b)   Bid four-card suits up the ladder.
  c)   Bid three of partner's minor with five or more.

6. Three of partner's minor.

7. You are saying you have NO FOUR-CARD MAJOR.

8. LIMIT BIDS ARE NOT FORCING.

9. Look for a 4-4 major suit fit (or better). Eight cards is a fit.

10.
  a)   Bid your long suit.
  b)   Bid four-card suits up the ladder.
  c)   Bid 2 NT showing your MAXI responding hand and no four-card major.
  d)   Bid the other minor and raise opener's suit to the three-level on the next round of bidding.

11. FORCING BIDS: a) non-limit bids   b) Jump bids in a new suit
12. NON-FORCING BIDS: a) limit bids   b) Game bids
13. A ROUND is complete when each person at the table has had one turn to bid.

WHAT DO YOU KNOW?   Page 114

PART A: Mini Responding Hands (6-9 HCP)

1. 2♣   LIMIT
2. 1♠   FORCING
3. 1◇   FORCING
4. 1 NT   LIMIT
5. 1◇   FORCING
6. 2♡   LIMIT
7. 2♠   LIMIT
8. 1 NT   LIMIT
9. 1 NT   LIMIT

PART B: Medium Responding Hands (10-12 HCP)   Page 115

1. 3♠   LIMIT
2. 3♡   LIMIT
3. 1♠   FORCING
4. 1◊   FORCING
5. 2◊   FORCING
6. 1◊   FORCING
7. 1◊   FORCING
8. 1♠   FORCING
9. 2◊   FORCING
10. 2♡ FORCING

PART C: Maxi Responding Hands (13 or more HCP)   Page 116

1. 4♠   LIMIT
2. 1♠   FORCING
3. 2 NT FORCING (no four-card major)
4. 2◊   FORCING (explore for a 4-4 major suit fit)
5. 2♡   FORCING
6. 2◊   FORCING (bid your long suit)
7. 2 NT FORCING (balanced hand, no four-card major)
8. 2♣   FORCING. Plan to bid diamonds at your next turn to show your fit.
9. 2 NT FORCING (no four-card major)

PART D: More Responses to 1-Level Openings   Page 118

1. a) LIMIT BID   6-9 points and three or more hearts
   b) LIMIT BID   10-12 points and three or more hearts
   c) LIMIT BID   6-9 points, no fit, and no four-card spade suit
   d) FORCING   13+ points, no fit and no four-card spade suit
   e) GAME and LIMIT BID 13+ points and a fit.
2. a) LIMIT BID   6-9 points, no four-card suit other than clubs, no five-card fit
   b) FORCING   EXPLORE, six or more points, four or more spades
   c) FORCING   13+ points, no four-card major, no five-card fit
   d) LIMIT BID   6-9 points, no four-card major, five or more clubs
   e) LIMIT BID   10-12 points, no four-card major, five or more clubs
3. a) FORCING   EXPLORE, six or more points, four or more spades
   b) FORCING   10 or more points, four or more clubs
   c) LIMIT   6-9 points, no four-card major
   d) LIMIT   6-9 points, five or more diamonds, no four-card major
4. a) LIMIT   10-12 points, three or more spades
   b) FORCING   10 or more points, five or more hearts. No support for spades.

SPECIAL NOTE: If you have only four hearts, you would also have either four clubs or four diamonds! We know this because if you don't have three spades, and you have only four hearts then you MUST have at least four cards in one of the minors in order to have 13 cards in your hand! AND we bid four-card suits UP THE LADDER, THEREFORE:

If the bidding goes   1♠   2♡

you must have five or more hearts.

  c)   GAME and LIMIT BID   13+ points and a fit
  d)   LIMIT   6-9 points and a fit
  e)   LIMIT   6-9 points and no fit
  f)   FORCING   10 or more points, four or more clubs

BRIDGE ART   Page 125

EXAMPLE	EXAMPLE
1 NT	1 NT
2♣	2♣
2♡	2♢
Three rounds	Three rounds
4♡	3 NT

WHAT DO YOU KNOW?   Page 126
PARTNER OPENS 1 NT

1.   2♠   NO ZONE HAND with a five-card suit. Opener will pass.
2.   PASS NO ZONE HAND with no five-card suit.
3.   2♣   STAYMAN, looking for a 4-4 major suit fit.
4.   2♣   STAYMAN. Plan to bid spades at your next turn to INVITE.
5.   2 NT   INVITE. No four-card major, balanced hand.
6.   2♣   STAYMAN and then bid hearts, showing a five-card or longer suit and an INVITE HAND.

WHAT IS YOUR STAYMAN RESPONSE?   Page 127
1.   2 NT   INVITE   You don't have a 4-4 spade fit.
2.   2 NT   INVITE   You didn't find a 4-4 heart fit.
3.   2♠   INVITE   Show a five-card or longer suit.
4.   2 NT   INVITE   You didn't find a 4-4 major suit fit.

THE WHOLE HAND   Page 128

1.
North	East	South	West
Pass	Pass	1 NT	Pass
2♣	Pass	2♡	Pass
3♡	Pass	4♡	Pass
Pass	Pass		

FINAL CONTRACT: 4♡

3.
North	East	South	West
	Pass	Pass	1 NT
Pass	2♣	Pass	2♢
Pass	3 NT	Pass	Pass
Pass			

FINAL CONTRACT: 3 NT

2.
North	East	South	West
			Pass
1 NT	Pass	3 NT	Pass
Pass	Pass		

FINAL CONTRACT: 3 NT

4.
North	East	South	West
		Pass	1 NT
Pass	2♣	Pass	2♢
Pass	2♠	Pass	4♠
Pass	Pass	Pass	

FINAL CONTRACT: 4♠

WHAT DO YOU KNOW?   Page 131
RESPONDING TO 1 NT WITH A GAME FORCE HAND

1. 3 NT Shows a balanced hand, 10 or more points, and no four-card major.
2. 2♣ STAYMAN searching for a 4-4 spade fit.
3. 4♡ YOU KNOW YOU HAVE A FIT so just bid game.
4. 5♣ YOU KNOW YOU HAVE A FIT and, with a singleton, you don't want to bid 3 NT.
5. 4♠ Partner has answered your STAYMAN bid by showing four spades. Now you know you have a 4-4 spade fit.
6. 3 NT Partner has responded to your STAYMAN bid by saying he has no four-card major. Without a 4-4 spade fit, you must bid 3 NT.
7. 3♠ JUMP BID your five-card major to show a game force hand.

WHAT DO YOU KNOW?   Page 135
RESPONDING TO 1 NT WITH A SLAM HAND

1. 4 NT LIMIT, showing your 16-17 HCP and no four-card major.
2. 2♣ STAYMAN, first looking for your 4-4 heart fit.
    If partner shows four hearts—jump to 5♡.
    If partner doesn't show four hearts—jump to 4 NT.
3. 5♡ INVITE SLAM. You have found your 4-4 fit.
4. 4 NT LIMIT showing your 16-17 HCP and no fit.
5. 6♠ You have found a fit and you have enough points to bid slam.
6. 3♠ FORCING. Jump in your five-card major to force partner to either show you a fit or bid 3 NT.
    If he shows a fit, bid 6♠.
    If he doesn't show a fit, bid 6 NT.
7. 6 NT Partner has told you he doesn't have a spade fit.

REVIEW   Page 137
RESPONDING WITH A MINI HAND (6-9 HCP)   Page 137

1. 2♠ LIMIT, showing a fit.
2. 1♠ FORCING, showing a four-card or longer major.
3. 1 NT LIMIT, showing no four-card major.
4. 1♡ FORCING, showing four or more hearts.
5. 1♠ FORCING. Bid your five-card suit first.
6. 2♡ LIMIT showing your fit.
7. 1 NT LIMIT. You can't bid 2♢ because a response on the two-level promises 10 or more points.
8. 1♢ FORCING. Bid your four-card suits up the ladder.

RESPONDING WITH A MEDIUM HAND (10-12 HCP)   Page 138

1. 3♡   LIMIT, showing a fit.
2. 2◇   FORCING. Bid your four-card suits up the ladder.
3. 2◇   FORCING, showing 10 or more points.
4. 2♣   FORCING. Bid your four-card suits up the ladder.
5. 1♠   EXPLORE for your 4-4 major suit fit.
6. 3♡   LIMIT, showing a fit.
7. 1♡   FORCING. Bid your long suit.
8. 3♠   LIMIT, showing a fit.
9. 3♡   LIMIT, showing a fit.
10. 1♡   FORCING. Bid your long suit first.

RESPONDING WITH A MAXI HAND (13 + HCP)   Page 139

1. 4♠   GAME. SHOW YOUR FIT.
2. 1♡   FORCING. Bid your long suit.
3. 1◇   FORCING. Bid your four-card suits up the ladder.
4. 2 NT   FORCING, showing a MAXI responding hand and no four-card major.
5. 1♠   FORCING. EXPLORE for a major suit fit.
6. 2◇   FORCING. Bid your long suit.
7. 1♡   FORCING. EXPLORE for a major suit fit.
8. 2◇   FORCING. Bid your four-card suits up the ladder.
9. 4♡   SHOW YOUR FIT.
10. 1◇   FORCING. Plan to make a JUMP BID in clubs at your next turn to show your fit and lots of points.

RESPONDING TO 1 NT OPENINGS   Page 141

1. 2◇   NO ZONE HAND, showing five or more diamonds and fewer than eight points.
2. PASS NO ZONE HAND, showing no five-card or longer suit and less than eight points.
3. 2♣   STAYMAN, looking for a 4-4 major suit fit.
4. 2 NT   INVITE, showing 8-9 points and a balanced hand.
5. 4♡   GAME, showing at least six hearts.
6. 2 NT   INVITE, with no four-card major.
7. 4♡   GAME. You know you have at least a 6-2 heart fit.
8. 3 NT   GAME. You know you have no 4-4 major suit fit because of partner's answer to Stayman.
9. 3♠   JUMP BID your five-card major to show your suit and to force to game.
10. 4♠   You have found a 4-4 spade fit and you have enough points to bid game.
11. 4 NT   You have enough points (16-17) to INVITE SLAM and you have no 4-4 major suit fit so invite slam in NT.
12. 4 NT   Opener has denied three spades so INVITE SLAM (16-17) in NT.
13. 5♠   You have found a fit so INVITE SLAM in spades.
14. 4 NT   INVITE SLAM. You have a balanced 16-17 HCP.
15. 5◇   Showing a six-card or longer suit.

TEST YOURSELF   Page 158

1. A rebid is the second bid made by either opener or responder.
2. a) No Chance for Game
   b) Invite to Game
   c) Bid to Game
   d) Invite to Game
   e) Bid to Game
   f) Invite to Slam
   g) Bid to Game
   h) Invite to Slam
   i) Bid to Slam
3. a Rebid NT without a jump.
   b) Raise partner's suit one-level (with a four-card fit).
   c) Rebid your major suit (with six or more cards)
   d) Rebid your minor suit (with five or more cards)

   a) Raise partner's 1 NT response to 2 NT.
   b) If responder bid two of your suit, bid three of the suit.
   c) Raise partner's new suit two levels with four cards in that suit.

   a) Jump raise partner's 1 NT response to 3 NT.
   b) If partner raised your major to the two-level, jump to game.
   c) Jump raise partner's new suit to game with four cards in that suit.
   d) Jump bid in NT.
4. a) Raise the suit to the three-level.
   b) Raise to 2 NT.
5. a) MINI + MEDIUM INVITE TO GAME.
   b) MEDIUM + MAXI INVITE TO SLAM.
6. a) MINI shows a fit by raising the suit one level.
   b) MEDIUM shows a fit by raising the suit two level.
   c) MAXI shows fit by raising the suit to game.

   a) MINI shows a fit by raising the suit to the two-level.
   b) MEDIUM shows a fit by raising the suit to the three-level.
   c) MAXI shows a fit by raising the suit to game.
7. BID FOUR-CARD SUITS UP THE LADDER.
8. You are saying you have one more card in that suit than you promised the first time you bid it.
9. The bidding should keep on going until either opener or responder has LIMITED his hand (at such time you make a decision as to where the bidding should stop) OR until GAME or SLAM has been bid.

1. OVERCALL   1 ♡

2. DOUBLE   For Takeout   You have no five-card suit BUT you have a fit for any suit partner might bid.

3. OVERCALL   1 NT   When you overcall 1 NT you are showing the same kind of hand you would have when you open 1 NT—15-17 points and no five-card major. BUT—you should also have an honor card in the suit OPENER bid.

4. OVERCALL   1 ♡   With two five-card suits, always bid the HIGHER RANKING SUIT FIRST.

5. OVERCALL   1 ♠

6. PASS   You don't have enough points to bid anything.

7. OVERCALL   1 ♡   Bid your long suit.

8. OVERCALL   1 ♡   Show your five-card major.

9. OVERCALL   1 ♠   Even though you don't have very many points, overcalling 1 ♠ works well because:

    a) You have the ace and king so you don't mind if partner leads spades.

    b) You have only one club so you will be able to TRUMP all their club tricks after the first if the contract is in your suit.

    c) You are bidding spades which takes up their bidding space—it will be hard for the responder to show his hearts if he has only 6-9 points, because he doesn't have enough points to bid on the two-level.

10. DOUBLE   For Takeout   Even though you have five diamonds you would rather DOUBLE to see if you and partner have a MAJOR SUIT FIT. Besides, you don't have a very good diamond suit and you don't really want partner to lead diamonds.

JUDE GOODWIN and **DON ELLISON** have been actively involved in the organization and promotion of bridge for many years, running tournaments, executive boards, clubs and classes.

Don, a Silver Life Master, has played bridge for 25 years starting at the age of 13. Currently working as a building designer and draftsman, Don teaches and plays bridge in Rossland, B.C.

Jude, a Bronze Life Master, and relative newcomer to the game, has played for nine years. She is well known, however, for her cartoon illustrations seen monthly in the ACBL *Bulletin* and published in her first book, *Table Talk.* She has also illustrated other bridge books *(Beginning Bridge Complete*—M. Penick and *Adventures in Duplicate*—Edith McMullin) is editor of the Vancouver *Matchpointer* and all District 19 Regional Newsletters and currently works as a free-lance graphic designer out of Vancouver, B.C.

Both Don and Jude have numerous sectional and regional titles and have played as a successful partnership for many years. The combination of Don's technical knowledge and broad experience and Jude's creative insight and fresh approach have produced a straightforward, entertaining learn and play manual with an emphasis on logic and fun.

PANDO PUBLICATIONS

TEACH ME TO PLAY: A FIRST BOOK OF BRIDGE
by Jude Goodwin and Don Ellison
$10.95

An introduction to the game of bridge designed for 8-14 year olds. Forget the heavy tomes and complex explanations. *Teach Me To Play* makes learning the game of bridge fun and easy for anyone. An Activity-Book filled with illustrations, fun pages, puzzles and projects keeps the up-and-coming bridge player fascinated throughout.

You start to play cards after just a few pages—after all, the fun of bridge is in the playing.

You will learn
— HOW TO BID
— HOW TO PLAY A HAND AS DECLARER
— HOW TO DEFEND

BRIDGE FROM THE TOP
by Marshall Miles
$11.95

— What conventions do you play after partner has opened 1 NT?
— Is a Forcing Club System best for you?
— Which conventions are best for Slam Bidding? Competitive Bidding? Game-Forcing Raises? Cue Bidding? and much more.

Do you find it difficult to choose among the huge variety of conventions and systems in the game of bridge? Then *Bridge From The Top* will be an invaluable guide for you. Mr. Miles evaluates most of the conventions and systems in use by experts and non-experts today and recommends those that have been proven to be most effective.

A complete guide for the player who wants to win.

JOURNALIST LEADS
by Lawrence Rosler and Jeff Rubens
$8.95

Your partner leads the ◇2 against a 4♡ contract. Dummy has the ◇J94. You have the ◇AKQ7. You quickly win the ◇Q and A. Now you have a problem. Will the ◇K cash or will declarer trump the third round of diamonds? You don't know. The problem is that your partner will lead the deuce from either three to the ten or from four to the ten and you have no way to know.

Your partner leads the ♡2 against a 3 NT contract. Dummy has two small. You have the ♡A63 and win the ace. Should you continue the suit? You should if partner has something like the ♡KJ92. You should shift if partner has something like the ♡10872.

Against a 4♠ contract your partner leads the ♣K. Dummy has the ♣J106. You have the ♣A9832. You play the nine and partner continues with the ♣Q. Do you overtake with your ace to give partner a ruff or do you play the deuce to avoid establishing dummy's jack? You should overtake if partner has a doubleton but you must play low if partner started with three clubs.

Problems like these are a nightmare for every bridge player. Playing standard lead methods there are no right answers. The problem is that standard lead methods do give the leader's partner the most important information. *Journalist Leads* solves these and many other problem situations. These methods have been tested and played by thousands of players from neophytes to world champions.

Pando Publications
540 Longleaf Drive
Roswell, Georgia 30075
(404) 587-3363

Date _____

Order Number _____

Name _____ Phone _____

Address _____ City _____ State _____ Zip _____

TITLE-AUTHOR	QUANTITY	PRICE	AMOUNT
Teach Me To Play—Goodwin and Ellison		$10.95	
Bridge From The Top—Miles		11.95	
Journalist Leads—Rosler and Rubens		8.95	

DISCOUNTS
TAKE A 10% DISCOUNT ON
ORDERS OVER $25
TAKE A 20% DISCOUNT ON
ORDERS OVER $50

SHIPPING
For U.S.A. orders, please add
$1.00/book with a maximum of $2.00/order.
Outside the U.S.A., please add 40¢/book
with a minimum of $2.00/order.
Please add an additional $4.00 for
C.O.D. orders
Georgia residents, please add 5% sales tax.

Retail Total _____

Discount _____

Shipping _____

Taxes _____

Balance Due _____